ABOUT THE A

Huw Jones has been a s ... lified by the ECB Coaches Associ ...

He has played crick ... amateur cricketer, he played in three na ... is home cricket club, Ealing, winning two of the ... eer as a player and coach has taken him to Australia, Uga ... , South Africa, India, France and the USA.

Huw was raised in London, where he now lives. His passion for sport grew out of the games he played with his brother and friends in the small garden of his home and the parks of London.

He now coaches cricket and child athleticism in West London and feels passionately that sport is a key ingredient in a happy, healthy life for children.

For more information and updates:

http://www.spotlightsport.co.uk
huw@spotlightsport.co.uk

OFFLINE AND ACTIVE

HEALTHY BODIES / STRONG MINDS: BUILD YOUR CHILD'S RESILIENCE & CONFIDENCE THROUGH SPORT

HUW JONES

Editing & Design by Kate White
intheworkscoaching@gmail.com

For my parents, who encouraged me to play sport and enjoy an active and happy childhood.

INTRODUCTION

PREPARE YOUR CHILD FOR THE PATH,
DON'T PREPARE THE PATH FOR YOUR CHILD.

Our children are growing up in a different world to the one we knew. Technology now plays such a dominant role in the lives of young children that we often forget that they have never known a world without the Internet, iPads, social media and mobile phones.

While we all know the advantages technology has given us, we are just as aware of its negatives. We know that there is something not quite right about the way our children are growing up. Children now have only known a world of endless entertainment and distractions. Attention spans are shortening by the year. Social skills are on the decline due to lack of direct contact with other people. Young people are involved in far less physical activity. This has led to health problems and a crisis of childhood obesity in western cultures especially.

Think about how these modern technologies have gradually become a prominent part of modern life:

- The Internet has made constant entertainment easily available.
- Mobile phones and computers have become constant companions in how we organise our lives and keep up with people and global events. This means more time hunched over screens and less time out engaging with the real world.
- Computer games. We've seen a huge increase in children (and adults) playing computer games for hours on end. Programmers understand exactly what products they need to create to keep people hooked on the screen in front of them.
- Social media has connected people in a way we could never have previously imagined. Whilst there are many positives to these connections, we also see young people struggling with online bullying and a decrease in the general levels of self-esteem. Social media has also promoted a celebrity culture. It's not difficult to see that this has not been a positive model of the world to be presenting to our youth. Materialism, superficiality and negativity seem to be a constant on these channels.

I've coached children to play sport for 15 years. My work has taken me from the United Kingdom to Australia, Uganda, South Africa, India, France and The United States, where I have taught sport and encouraged children to learn to move correctly. In the last 5 years I have noticed a significant change in the children who attend my sports coaching sessions.

Suddenly I was seeing children who were struggling to run, balance, jump, or co-ordinate themselves effectively. It was not difficult to see what the cause of this was. Increasingly children were showing up with mobile phones and iPads to keep them occupied (and distracted) at every spare moment.

Each year I saw a noticeable decline in general co-ordination and body strength and an increase in the amount of time the children would use and talk about technology. For me, the tipping point to consider ways to solve this problem came in the summer of 2018, during a children's holiday camp I was running in London. I looked around the lunch hall and saw every one of the kids between the ages of 11 and 15 looking silently at their mobile phones. The entire one hour lunch break was spent furthering their progress on the computer game *Fortnight*. These children were able to log in to their accounts and continue the games they had been playing at home. Interestingly, the children younger than 11 were outside playing hide and seek or whichever ball game they had created amongst themselves. Fortunately, younger children haven't yet been given their own phones to distract them. Children need to be outside and playing with other children and it's clear we're starting to lose our grip on this fundamental principle.

Another concern is the obvious shortening of attention spans that is very noticeable in people of all ages. The worry is that young people will grow up having never learnt how to stick at things and focus for any period of time. I've noticed a real lack of drive and determination in this generation.

By relying on electronics to entertain themselves, young people are not developing the same imagination that was needed in previous times. With endless opportunities to fill their time, there is no space to think for themselves and develop practical skills.

While some technology can develop aspects of creativity in younger people, there is a worry that purely consuming entertainment and playing games can lead to young people wasting their key developmental years. Parents are reporting difficulties in limiting screen time – there seems to be a constant battle going on in many households with concerned and frustrated parents trying to pry their sons and daughters away from their constant need to be online and connected to their favourite channels. Often parents are lost for ideas in how to stop the tide of technology taking over their children's lives.

Technology and the Internet are here to stay – they are a key part of all of our lives. However, I have seen first-hand the negative effects they are having on our children. I have written this book to present an alternative. I believe encouraging a child to enjoy playing sport is a crucial counter-balance to the problems we are seeing in young people's development today.

Sport was the main interest I had growing up. I just wanted to be outside playing and practicing whichever sport had captured my imagination at the time. It kept me physically active, helped me make friends, and developed my confidence and ability to play in a team. I don't think I could have learnt those skills in any other way.

Not only is sport a natural way to stay healthy, it's also an excellent training ground for a child to learn character traits that can serve them later in life. I believe sport can teach your child the important ability to handle challenge and failure in their life. To achieve anything meaningful, they will need to persist and sport can be an excellent way to learn to push on through difficulties. By seeing their lives as a constant stream of instant pleasures and entertainments, we may be setting our children up for unhappy lives. I believe we need to encourage the attitude of taking on challenges, risking failure, and persisting when things are difficult to achieve greater pleasures than just the fast entertainment that the Internet can provide.

Sport can teach your child who they are as a person. They can learn the strengths and weaknesses of their personality and natural abilities. By testing themselves they can see where they stand and what they need to improve upon. Without any tests, how can we truly find out what we're capable of?

Play – be it children playing with friends or parents or in organised sports sessions – is also the best way for children explore their potential and recover from life's upsets. It is an essential part of their enjoyment of life. There should always be opportunities for children to play on their own or with friends their age. As parents we can give our children ideas about how they can play, and also teach them how they can do so effectively by putting the right tools around them.

Playing with your child can build the connection between you and reduces the natural friction in the parent-child dynamic. As parents, you might miss your chance to connect with your children, due to the pressures of modern life – or because you are distracted by technology yourself. If you've lost connection with your child, play is perhaps the best way to rebuild that relationship.

We prepare children best by both nurturing them and challenging them. My metaphor for this combination is bricks and mortar; you can't build a strong wall with just one or the other. Children gain an inner strength—the mortar—from being loved and nurtured, having their needs met, knowing they are loved no matter what. They get a different kind of confidence—the bricks—from being challenged and playing their hardest.

Lawrence J. Cohen

There is no 'one size fits all' approach to bringing up children. Each child is unique and will have his/her own natural interests. However, we need our young people to have a desire to achieve and develop a winning mentality towards their lives. Settling for mediocrity is dangerous and can led to very dissatisfied adults. There is a danger that we are setting our children up to be totally unprepared for the real world when they leave us.

This book presents ideas of how to create some physical and social balance in the upbringing of our children and keep technology from taking on an unhealthy role in your child's development. I offer my own perspective on how sport can be incorporated into a child's development, both physically and as a tool for improving character traits

Chapter 1 delves into the world of the modern child, while Chapter 2 looks at how sport can give young people a purpose and a way to focus their minds in a healthy direction, and at the same time improve your child's health and physical development. Chapter 3 details the character development and social skills that can be learnt from playing sports in our younger years. Chapter 4 looks at how sport helps develop children's social skills. The last 3 chapters offer practical ways parents can encourage their child to be active, how to communicate effectively, and create a home that promotes physical activity.

My hope is that I can demonstrate to you the value in encouraging your child to enjoy sport. It's my view that sport is more important than ever in providing balance to young people's lives. Children need to feel secure and self-confident. We can help them get to that point by giving them the appropriate attention and taking interest in what they want to do. This way we allow them to explore rather than feeling the need to force them.

I hope you enjoy this perspective and that this book prompts you to think of ways your child can benefit from playing sport, being active, and developing themselves in the process!

IT'S EASIER TO BUILD STRONG CHILDREN
THAN IT IS TO REPAIR BROKEN MEN.

FREDERICK DOUGLAS (1817-1895)

1

UNDERSTANDING THE MODERN CHILD

Today's youth is rotten, evil, godless and lazy. It will never be what youth used to be, and it will never be able to preserve our culture.

Babylonian clay tablet, 1000 BC

Does that sound familiar? Older generations have always seen those following them as spoilt and lazy. It's easy to think that 'things were better in our day', that standards have slipped, that young people are less valuable to society or lacking the character traits of our generation.

We also all have ideas of how things 'should be' for children, ideas often shaped by our own upbringings and what we felt was right or wrong about what we experienced. If we had an overbearing parent, we might feel strongly that children need to be left alone to be themselves. If we felt we were left too much to our own devices, we may want to give our own children the guidance we felt we lacked and would have benefitted from.

Yet the world around us is constantly changing and evolving, meaning that we have to adapt our behaviour to these new conditions. It's essential that we understand that each generation of children grows up in unique circumstances. Learning to see our children's world through their eyes allows us as parents and teachers to understand the opportunities and stresses they face.

Our Children's World

Our natural tendency is to bring children into our adult world instead of being prepared to enter into theirs. We can't hope for our children to have the same lives we had. In fact, there are huge advantages to be had in growing up now. Access to knowledge and high-quality facilities have never been better. Some of the boys and girls I coach go on school trips to the UAE, South Africa, America, or other European countries. The opportunity to develop and pursue interests has never been easier, yet there are also many more distractions and opportunities to waste time.

To understand your child's world, look at how you are living now versus how things were just a few years ago. In many ways, life has become easier for the average person. Technology has brought a host of life-improving gadgets and services. We are just a few presses of a button away from a car pulling up to collect us or a meal being delivered to the front door. Every home has central heating and hundreds of television channels (as well as unlimited online content) to keep us occupied. We are rapidly solving a lot of problems and making our lives more comfortable.

At the same time, as technology solves one problem, it often creates others. And there may be a bigger question to ask: are we losing depth and meaning in our lives?

The Digital World: Pros & Cons

In many ways, our children are learning new digital skills that will be essential for their future. Watching a 3-year-old operate a smart phone or tablet is something to behold. These technical skills are allowing children to do new things and learn in innovative ways. The traditional teaching styles of books and blackboards have been replaced by iPads and the increasing use of virtual reality, which are proving to be excellent learning tools.

With the incredible amount of information available to them, children are able to delve deeply into topics that interest them. They can discover many new perspectives that weren't available to us. Even online gaming has some positive side effects, although I think we all know the problems here. These games and other online tools such as *YouTube* provide children opportunities to develop some creative ability in making videos and solving problems. And while social media receives a fair bit of criticism for its volatility and risks, studies have shown that it can develop some empathy in children, as it allows them to experience other people's stories, diverse cultures, and different ways of thinking.

Although we can all acknowledge the positives, it is difficult to argue against the idea that we are in an era of experimentation with our children. We don't yet know how this accelerated usage of technology will affect them. Many children are now developing addictions to technology. Parents complain that they struggle to control screen time with very angry and grumpy kids who want to get back to their latest game or *YouTube* channel. Social media has quickly become a prominent part of a lot people's lives, particularly for the younger generations.

According to studies, only one in 20 kids in the United States meets guidelines on sleep, exercise and screen time.

Knell, Durrand & Kohl

It's important to remember that young people today have never known a world without the internet or social media. This has increased the pressures on parents who must make sure their children are not exposed to the wrong things early in their lives. There are also worries about the behaviour of others online who can intimidate and bully their child before they are ready to handle it.

In a UK study of 14-17 year olds, teenagers were more than twice as likely to ever have been diagnosed with depression when accessing electronic devices for 7 hours or more per day.

Twenge & Campbell, 2018

A lot of things children are exposed to these days can be very harmful. A couple of years ago I was shocked to find out a few of the 10 year olds in my coaching group had seen the movie *The Wolf Of Wall Street* (an X-Rated movie, for those of you who have not seen it). These children had seen this movie through their parents' *Netflix* accounts. It's becoming harder to shelter children from accessing material not designed for them.

Parents are very concerned that their children are being exposed to things online that they are not prepared for. Even such seemingly 'safe' activities as online gaming can expose younger children to aggressive strangers who speak nastily to them. This is a scary world to be living in, especially in your own home. This kind of nastiness has become a way of life for a lot of children on platforms such as *WhatsApp* groups and *Twitter*.

With these safety concerns, many parents are limiting their child's independence. This very understandable fear for their children's safety is causing parents to shelter their children from what they perceive to be the harsh realities of the real world. In a 2013 study, two thirds of children reported that they had experienced negative incidences online. I would suggest that these days, that number may be higher.

Physical & Emotional Impacts

I worry about some of the children I see in my coaching. The enthusiasm for being outdoors and playing seems to be waning, and when I ask some of these children about their interests, they often don't have an answer other than 'playing computer games'. Without a doubt, children from Westernised countries are less physically developed and resistant to injury these days. Having not had the bumps and knocks that children of previous generations had, their bodies are fragile and oftentimes weak. I see a lot more physical injuries simply because children can't handle falling over or protect themselves from being bumped into by another child.

Our schools can often teach children lessons that don't apply to the real world. Well-intentioned ideas like 'participation trophies' are causing children to live artificial lives in many ways. As adults, no one is going to reward someone simply for showing up and not providing real value. We should teach our children that they need to strive and improve, not settle for mediocrity.

Emotionally, too, children are not as resilient as they used to be. It's become far more common to hear children complaining of tiredness or minor injuries than was previously the case. The phrase "I can't" has become very frequent and I'm sure is tiring for many teachers. Children really struggle these days when things don't go their way. I've seen schoolteachers allow children to win a competition simply because they don't want to deal with the backlash of a child who can't handle losing.

Parents, too, are a bit unsure how to go about things. When other parents around you act in a certain way, there is a pressure to 'keep up' and be seen to be doing the right thing. I've seen Dads competing with each other to be the most serious about their child's training to such an extent that we have to speak to them about disrupting the sports coaching sessions. Fathers will sit at the back of sports hall, often wearing full tracksuits, and watch every second of what their child is doing. This surveillance is not good for the child's enjoyment of play and general social development. We often see young children constantly looking over to their parents to receive acknowledgement for what they're doing instead of simply enjoying the sessions.

In perhaps the most comical instance I've experienced as a sports coach, I saw a father rush in to console his 11-year-old son who had been struck on the leg by a tennis ball. The panicked father ran into the centre of the sports hall to interrupt the session, then lifted and carried his inconsolable child away to the seating area where he rubbed and cradled the boy. The screaming continued for 3 or 4 minutes until the child realised no damage had been done at all. I sympathise with children when they are hurt, but circumstances like this are not good for a child. We need to teach them how to handle pain. How will they ever withstand something as simple as a dental appointment if they are hyper-sensitive to small amounts of pain?

Social media and technology is also affecting how our young people communicate. They are used to being in constant contact with people through devices. Psychologists are increasingly focussed on the problems associated with a lack of direct social contact among young people, and are starting to discuss mental disorders that are the consequence of social media usage. We are starting to understand that direct eye contact is a crucial factor in people feeling connected with others; without it they can feel lonely and unsure of themselves.

One mother made this comment on the *Netmums.com* forum:

> *He used some phrases like 'lost the motivation' to play his instrument and alluded to gaming as he has no life outside of school. I asked if he was depressed, he said not. I feel so sad that his world is so small and believe he is missing out on so much. I'm really worried that if we don't do something to change his behaviour now we'll have missed our chance and he won't have the skills to live a full, rounded and social life.*

Technology is actually changing the way our brains operate. By training it daily to be used to fast stimulation, our brains crave more. This is perhaps the main difference between children now and 20 years ago. Anyone working with children now will attest to this. In particular, there has been a major change in children's attention spans. I have noticed a significant change in the children I've coached. Children become bored a lot faster, and I've had to adapt my coaching methods to cater for this. Whereas I might have designed a training exercise to last 15 minutes, this is no longer effective. Now I design exercises that change every 5 minutes to ensure children don't get distracted and lose focus completely.

On average, children aged eight to 11 spend 3.6 hours a day glued to a TV or other electronic screens in the United States.

The Guardian, 2018

Life Impacts

With so much choice available to children these days, they tend to spread their attention and not focus properly on things that have real world value to them. I'm concerned that we are going to see a lot of young people emerging into adult life with no real idea what they want to do in life and what their real interests are. People need to have a healthy, positive focus. Without it, they drift into unhealthy distractions and addictions.

In addition, if we grow up lacking any feeling of accomplishment, we can feel we are wasting our time. When we look back on our childhood, we like to be able to identify what we actually did with our time. I would suggest 'I played computer games and watched *YouTube* videos' will not be the answer we want!

We are seeing increasing cases of depression, not just in young people, but in people of all ages. While social media and the internet connect people more than ever, we often do so in isolation. Humans evolved to interact with each other in person, face to face. Something as simple as eye contact is crucial to our mental health and self-esteem. In our efforts to make our young people's lives comfortable, we may be harming them in the worst way possible: by isolating them from healthy interactions with others.

Another worrying trend is young people's lack of interest in learning. They may do what they need to pass school exams, but don't seem to think that older people have anything of value to teach them. Many times, I've noticed looks of disinterest from children when teachers genuinely try and help them. We need to encourage them to be open to learning and to show them how much benefit they will receive from being open minded about improving themselves. Not everything in their lives will be achieved by tapping a few buttons on a screen.

There is also a noticeable lack of respect for authority in children now. This has become an undeniable problem with children in western society. School teachers I've spoken to have all confirmed this, and in my coaching work I'm finding it to be an increasing problem. Trying to discipline children, or even expecting basic respect from children, has become increasingly challenging. How do you teach a child the necessary skills they need when there's a basic lack of respect for teachers and people in authority?

That said, sometimes children are difficult because they want to connect with you more. I've started to see difficult children in a different light recently. I now believe that children often misbehave because they don't feel connected to their parents.

This disconnection creates an unsettled child who seeks attention by acting up. While it's easy to look at these children and see their flaws, we also need to think about the environment they are growing up in.

Another key issue is character building. This is not a topic discussed very often these days, but is integral to how children learn to treat themselves and others. As parents, we can expect that certain character traits are not being developed in their current environment. How can a child develop resilience or determination if those character traits have never been instilled in their childhood? We can't simply expect that these traits will 'turn on' naturally as our children reach 18 years of age. They must be cultivated over time with the correct challenges and influences.

A Way Forward

If the spirit of the times is like a tide or stream,
better to find a way to gently redirect it,
instead of fighting its direction.

Robert Greene, *The Laws of Human Nature*

The online world is increasingly becoming the more dominant world for young people: being offline is a now rare thing. There's no point resisting these new developments: *YouTube*, mobile phones, social media and unlimited digital entertainment are here to stay, but it does mean that our children are not used to being without stimulation.

The way forward? Adapt! Things need to be fresh and engaging. We must show children that the offline world has far more to offer in terms of depth and enjoyment of life. It seems obvious to me that children these days need to have solid, balanced lives that are ***offline*** so that they don't take the online world too seriously. While being outside playing will never be a totally danger-free scenario, we can at least see that the online world contains many more concerning issues. Children who have a healthy 'real world' life, have a far healthier outlook and less fear. The world is a friendlier place for them.

I think we all believe that a childhood should be about physical play. A happy child is engaged with the world and fascinated by what he or she is learning every day in the real world. We need to recapture what has been lost and return our children to a more natural way of behaving.

In the next chapter, we dive into how sport can give your children a purpose and focus their minds in a healthy direction, and at the same time improve their health and physical development.

2

HOW SPORT CAN IMPROVE YOUR CHILD'S HEALTH & PHYSICAL DEVELOPMENT

Obesity rates among 2- to 19-year-olds have risen from 10 percent in the late 1980s and early 1990s to 18.5 percent in 2016, according to US studies.

Wang & Lim, 2012

The Physical Health of Young People

We all know the benefits of physical exercise. I think we all know, too, that physical health is on the decline. Obesity, even in children, is a massive concern in western cultures.

In previous eras, playing outside was the most fun a child could have. Today, safety concerns and increasing use of technology keep children indoors, which means they aren't getting the opportunity to challenge their bodies to run, jump, and move. In addition, they aren't getting enough fresh air and sunlight. We humans need sunlight to be healthy. Exposure to the sun elevates our vitamin D levels, which are vital for a range of health benefits. We also benefit from a more positive mood when we've been outside and exposed to the elements.

Although it's essential for young people's health and general physical well-being that they get outdoors and play, cultural trends tend to push against this. One effect is a decline in the physical mobility of children, something I have seen in my own coaching. Often 10 year olds show up for our sessions almost dragging their bodies with them. Their posture looks slouched and some children are visibly overweight and unable to run or jump. Many children come to sports sessions wearing expensive shoes and tracksuits, but are lacking in even the most basic of movement patterns.

A couple of years ago a 10 year old child arrived late for one of our sports sessions. He had his phone to his ear and a Costa Coffee bag in his hand as he slowly dragged both himself and his kit bag toward where we were playing. He gave me a nod as if to say, 'be with you in a minute'. I could only laugh. He looked like a 45 year old executive.

Without the basic ability to move our bodies, we are susceptible to physical injury and will not build the strength and coordination to handle the practical tasks we need to perform in our lives. Unfortunately, physical education in schools can be very poor. We can't expect our children will get adequate exercise and learn to move their bodies correctly simply because their school has a Physical Education class once a week. Other than these very basic classes, some children grow up with no physical activity at all in their lives.

Another clear trend is a lack of physical strength in children. When I first started coaching, we would often punish a misbehaving child with a demand for '10 press ups'. These days I very rarely see a child who can do even one proper press up. They don't have the strength in their arms and shoulders to push their bodies off the ground. And this is not a minority of children, but almost all children under the age of 13!

I also get regular complaints during the warm-up segment of our sessions. Children often say they're tired or need water just 5 minutes into a session. This is a worrying development and, I would suggest, something you should be concerned about for your child.

Through my sports coaching, I've come to realise the importance of a child learning physical movements by playing active games. A child's ability to learn to run and jump properly can only be developed through repeated activity and regular play. Without adequate play in their lives, we create a Catch 22 situation: children are less co-ordinated to play sport so they are less likely to enjoy it. If they don't enjoy sport, they will make no effort to play at all.

The way forward is to give children a foundation of physical ability by creating fun opportunities to physically play, so that sport is actually pleasurable for them. Trying to get children to exercise without any fun and play is very difficult. We have to make things enjoyable or we will encounter resistance every step of the way – something that parents know well! By playing sport, we teach children to move correctly while they enjoy being active and exercising. In addition, physical challenges give children a chance to learn what their bodies are capable of. One reason teenagers seek out trouble and dangerous activities is their need to explore and see what they can do at new phases of their physical development.

In the long-term, the natural result will be an adult who enjoys exercising. Not everyone will have physically active jobs or play sport in their adult lives. However, I do believe that everyone should have a positive relationship with their bodies, be able to move well, and be functional in how they move. We all see adults who are physically inactive suffering from aches and pains that are very difficult to live with. I believe the first step in avoiding these issues is to develop healthy movement patterns in our early years so that our bodies operate effectively.

What Sport Can Do for Your Child's Physical Health

Learning to move well is a key part of child development, as important as learning to read and write. Developing adequate co-ordination and a body that can protect itself from injury will serve your child well in their future years, no matter what their later interests are.

Sport is the most natural way to learn to move well and develop effective co-ordination. It gives an excellent grounding and physical foundation that will help children throughout their lives. Being physically fit is not just about making sure we don't become overweight – we also need to have bodies that are pain free and resistant to injury. These days we have problems where children are easily injured due to lacking this basic 'physical education'.

Consider the worrying scenario of being mugged or attacked in the street – something that could happen to any of us. Without the ability to run properly or move out of the way, we can't avoid danger. By being active in our youth, we learn to effectively move our bodies in the ways that we need. If we trip over, we can recover our balance instead of falling and doing damage to our bodies.

The physical exercises involved in playing sport have a range of positive side-effects. Some of the immediate benefits include being better able to cope with stress, mental health, and depression; improved sleep; and a safe and positive way to tension and aggression.

Between 2010 and 2015, the number of teens in the US who felt useless and joyless, surged 33% in large surveys. Teen suicide attempts increased 23%. **Jean M. Twenge, 2017**

Playing sport is a great 'stress buster' for young people. We often forget that life can be quite traumatic as young children transform into adults – so much physical and psychological change is taking place. Mental health has become a serious issue and young people in particular have been the focus of much concern. There are increasing reports of depression linked to technology usage.

Just being outside in the fresh air is good for the mind, and some doctors now prescribe going outdoors as a way to cope with stress and depression. Loneliness and depression can come from feeling isolated and disconnected. By being outside, playing and interacting with others, children can fill their basic need for connection, as well as benefiting from increased serotonin levels in their brains, which improves mood. It's a much-needed antidote to children firing up the pleasure chemicals in their brains (dopamine) in short spikes on digital devices, only to return to a dissatisfied state when away from them. Aside from losing out on face-to-face interaction, children can easily become addicted to the stimulation provided by social media, mobile phones and other digital tech.

> It's estimated that two-thirds of teenagers take their phones to bed in the UK and around 30% sleep with them. 36% of teens say they wake up in the night at least once to check their phones.
>
> Twenge & Campbell, 2018

By sheltering our children from playing outside, we harm them in ways we may not even consider. Our immune systems need to be exposed to the cold air and dirt of the outdoors. Without enough exposure to these elements, young people can develop fragile immune systems that can't withstand being outside at all, leaving them vulnerable to unnecessary illnesses and medical conditions (even when they become adults).

Outdoor play also helps with temperature regulation. These days, children often report that they are either too hot or too cold. They are very sensitive because they spend a lot of time inside in temperature-controlled houses and school classrooms. Without the ability to handle different climates, your child is going to be greatly limited in where they can go in the world and what they can explore. I often tell the children I coach that 25 degrees Celsius is not hot by the standards of a lot of other countries, but in their minds, it's unbearable! We need to encourage our children to bear different weather conditions and have the determination to continue.

What's more, sleep quality can be negatively affected by technology and a lack of outdoor play. These, combined with exposure to artificial lights before bedtime, are causing restless sleep for young people. By playing outside, getting some fresh air, and dare I say running around a bit, your child can sleep better and achieve more rest.

And last but not least, by physically exercising, your child can become more pleasant with you because they let off steam and any frustrations on the sports ground. Often difficult behaviour is just tension that hasn't been released. Even games like tag and play fighting with other children can teach them physical confidence and an understanding of how to use their bodies safely. Both boys and girls like this type of play.

Encouraging your child to play sport has many positive short-term and long-term effects. In the short-term, your child will naturally get more physical activity: they will be healthier, far less prone to being overweight, and will develop confidence in their bodies' physical ability to move properly. In the long-term, by developing their sports performance, your child will also build good habits that will form the foundation of a healthy lifestyle.

I'm sure you don't need too much convincing about the undeniable physical benefits of playing sport. I believe there is far more to be gained as well. We'll now explore the character development and social skills that can be learnt from playing sports in our younger years.

> For adults, play means leisure, but for children, play is more like their job. Unlike many of us adults, they usually love their work and seldom want a day off. Play is also children's main way of communicating, of experimenting, and of learning.
>
> **Lawrence J. Cohen**

3

HOW SPORT DEVELOPS CHARACTER IN YOUNG PEOPLE

CHARACTER IS THE MENTAL AND MORAL QUALITIES OF AN INDIVIDUAL.

Character

Character is a word that seems to have gone out of fashion, particularly with regard to children's development. Previous generations emphasised the importance of building character traits like perseverance, toughness, resilience and determination as being key ingredients in a successful person. It's my belief that old-fashioned character traits are as important as ever – perhaps more so. In an attempt to be progressive and forward thinking, we may well be denying our children the opportunity to face challenges and learning experiences that existed for very good reasons.

Adults with strong character function far more effectively. They find it easy to meet new people and they get more respect from their peers. By being at ease with their place in the world, they relax other people around them. People like to give these types responsibility as they seem to 'have a level head on their shoulders.' I'm sure we can all recall meeting people of strong character and we know instinctively that this can only be developed through experience. Without a strong character, many of our strengths can't flourish.

So how can character be developed?

A person's character is formed in childhood. Issues that surface later on are mostly issues that were formed during a dysfunctional childhood. Problems with addiction, for example, can often be a compensation for problems a person hasn't resolved from their upbringing. Having to deal with such emotional discomfort as adults is a distraction from moving forward in our lives effectively and building healthy relationships with others.

As a parent, you have a huge influence on how your child will develop. Both your example and your communication will affect how your child acts and thinks when they are an adult. What type of adult would you like your child to be? Will it be better for them to have resilience and determination, or to be fragile and vulnerable when they are alone and without your support in the real world?

The temptation to choose an easy, comfortable life is greater than ever. Everything happens so quickly now and young people expect results immediately. It's only natural in a world where they can press some buttons on a phone and a meal will be hand delivered to them. Why develop patience when everything happens on demand and instantly? Taking time and waiting for things to unfold is seen as boring and unnecessary. Our children are growing up in this comfortable, instant gratification world with lots of digital 'toys' to keep them occupied and entertained. Computers can also be great learning tools, but they prevent children experiencing any type of boredom and thus get in the way of them getting up and making things happen for themselves. Worse, young people are losing the desire to learn new practical skills and develop their body physically.

This is where perseverance, toughness, resilience and determination can make all the difference in building strong, capable children who are well prepared for life's challenges and opportunities. I find sport can provide wonderful role models for children to develop these traits.

> Now some parents think their job is to protect children from every hurt and danger. But that is not possible, and not desirable. What we need to give them instead is the strength, the confidence, the skills, and the connection with others that allows them to cope with being hurt, and even grow from it.
>
> Lawrence J. Cohen

Building Character

If your child is to become skilful or effective at anything, they will need to persevere. They will need to be able to handle failure and conflicts with people. Will they learn these traits by living in a comfortable bubble where they are never exposed to challenge and difficulty?

I've seen many parents who have the best intentions for their children but feel the need to step in and solve all of their problems for them. It's not uncommon these days to see a child walking ahead of their parent whilst their mother or father carries their school bag or sports kit and hand delivers it to them when they've arrived for their session. I've also had situations where the parent will walk into the middle of sports sessions with a snack for their child or to stand with them whilst they are playing sport (we will cover 'Helicopter parents' in Chapter 7).

I remember a particularly shy and anxious 8 year old who joined our holiday camps. On the first morning he was nervous, I had to walk him away from the group to ask him what was wrong. He said he was scared and that he didn't know anyone. I think everyone knows this feeling from childhood and it is a common scenario on holiday camps where a child has to spend all day with new people in a new place. The best thing an adult can do for a child in a circumstance like this is to encourage them, give them confidence, and let them know that it is fine that they feel this way. You don't remove the child and send them home. You help them push through their anxiety and develop confidence as a consequence. By the end of the first day, this boy was feeling comfortable and his anxiety had greatly reduced. By day 2, he'd settled in and started to make friends.

By not allowing young people to experience any difficulties, we make them soft and vulnerable even to minor challenges later in their lives. Sickness and injury are far more common these days because children are not developing to be robust, both mentally and physically. Just as an immune system strengthens from being exposed to some uncomfortable environments, so must your child's character. By sheltering your child too much and stepping in at any sign of difficulty, you may be hindering their chance of thriving later in life. In the end, it might be the difficulties – rather than the comforts – that are of more value for your child.

> ARMED WITH A GROWTH MINDSET, SHE INTERPRETED FALLING DOWN NOT MERELY AS A MEANS OF IMPROVING, BUT AS EVIDENCE THAT SHE WAS IMPROVING. FAILURE WAS NOT SOMETHING THAT SAPPED HER ENERGY AND VITALITY, BUT SOMETHING THAT PROVIDED HER WITH AN OPPORTUNITY TO LEARN, DEVELOP, AND ADAPT.
>
> MATTHEW SYED

It's not uncommon for children these days to never attempt anything difficult, leaving them with no solid accomplishments. This lack of achievement can lead them into envying other people or becoming difficult socially as they try and compete with people in the wrong ways. They also become too brittle to take criticism, and the only way they feel they can 'measure up' is to cut others down with negativity. We see this kind of behaviour manifesting in the explosion of internet 'trolling', and it's a sign of a real weakness of character in society today.

No parent wishes difficulty on their child, but perhaps we can allow for some to be a natural part of growing up. By playing sport, this can be done in a controlled way. They can draw on tough experiences and form a character that stands them in great stead later on. Using sport as a tool for this learning can be very effective.

OUR LIFE INEVITABLY INVOLVES OBSTACLES, FRUSTRATIONS, PAIN AND SEPARATIONS. HOW WE COME TO HANDLE SUCH MOMENTS IN OUR EARLY YEARS PLAYS A LARGE ROLE IN THE DEVELOPMENT OF OUR OVERALL ATTITUDE TOWARD LIFE.

ROBERT GREENE, *THE LAWS OF HUMAN NATURE*

Resilience

I personally have learned many lessons from playing sport. It has allowed me to travel and has exposed me to many different environments which have developed my confidence in who I am. I was able to improve my leadership skills, deal with nerves, and learn to meet new people. Dealing with the pressure of sports matches has been an excellent way to develop determination and to not give up when things get difficult.

The social challenges of playing team sports also provide an excellent training ground for how to get on with people in an effective way and resolve differences. Competing with other teams can teach a young person how to effectively deal with people who try to bully them. This can be a key life skill that prevents people from becoming victims of aggressive behaviour from others, even in their adult lives. Just think of the many work scenarios your child might later find themselves in and the different personalities they will deal with.

By sheltering your child from discouragement and disappointment, you look after their short-term emotions to the detriment of their long-term development. Everyone will experience pain, frustration and difficulty. Why not naturally expose children, in a controlled way, to a little bit of challenge in preparation for this?

In the same way that physical exercise builds strong bodies, a young person's mind is stretched and strengthened through resistance and challenge. We cannot expect a strong mind if we never challenge it. A lot of young people want to avoid boredom, pain and adversity. You can't be good at anything that way. They must embrace pain and struggle as a means to get stronger, as part of the process of improvement.

You can even teach your child the beauty of things not going their way. Their failures can teach them lessons and make the wins even sweeter. A loss one week can spur on an even bigger win the following week or later in a season. Young people need to learn that there is no situation in their life that will be a constant stream of one win after another. At times, life gets hard for everyone; usually what gets us through is the commitment and determination to stick at it. Your child must learn this early and I believe sport is the perfect vehicle to do that.

In particular, it's important that we encourage young people to push through boredom. This is a real challenge these days as concentration spans become shorter and shorter. If your children are going to get good at anything in their lives, they will need to handle boredom and be able to carry on even when things aren't going their way. Sport can provide a chance for them to repeat an activity, get better at it, and see the results in front of their eyes. The physical satisfaction from hitting or catching a ball or running better can be a better thrill than any computer game. Without any electronic devices around them to distract their attention, children can develop more effective concentration from playing sport.

To get good at anything, your child will need a desire to keep going and persist. No one is above the process of overcoming challenge and obstacles in whatever they are trying to do.

Without a history of trying to achieve things, it makes it very difficult for a person to get started and go after something with confidence.

The ability to try new things and bounce back from disappointment is a major key to long-term success. By learning this in one way, we can transfer that strength of character to other endeavours. Setbacks and failures make people stronger when they learn the right mental approach. Disappointments can plant seeds for future success. The will to overcome must be learnt and emphasised in young people. Trying and failing is a far better feeling than not having the determination to try in the first place. It can do major damage to someone's self-esteem to know that they never attempted to do something or that they have waste their potential. Adults often look back on their childhoods and wish they had tried more things. Sport can be a great opportunity to try new things and learn about ourselves in our younger years.

Toughness: Handling Anxiety

PLAY CREATES AN OPPORTUNITY TO EXPRESS LOVE AND NURTURING, GENTLY REPAIRING THE WOUNDS OF EARLIER CONFLICTS OR UPSETS.

LAWRENCE J. COHEN

Perhaps the least fashionable word these days is 'toughness'. The idea of mental toughness does not get much emphasis in the education of our children. I think we'd all agree that adult life requires mental toughness. Things don't always go to plan and everyone's life involves failure at some point or another. To deprive your child of the opportunity to learn mental toughness can be setting them up for a bigger fall later in life. Without experiencing a few difficult but controlled failures in their childhood, young people may develop into adults who become overly emotional or difficult when things don't go their way. I believe sport can humble children and teach them that it's ok to fail. The sun will still come up tomorrow and provide them with another chance to try again. Sport can reinforce a positive mindset in people.

Sport is also a great way to help children confront their social fears, something we'll look at more fully in the next chapter. If they struggle with social anxiety, going to a sports club can be a good way to lean into that fear and develop the confidence they need. There is a lot of anxiety in young people these days. The news, social media and volatile global events loom larger in their lives than it may have during our childhoods, and they feel that the world can be a very scary place. While we may look at young people and feel their lives are easier, they are certainly feeling more anxiety than ever, and studies on teenage mental health support this.

If a child lowers their belief about what is possible for them and how much they can improve their situation, their self-esteem and ambition can really diminish. They start to believe that good things are possible for others but not for them. It's my understanding that this is what is causing an increase in anxiety and mental health issues in young people. The influence of social media exaggerates this feeling, as they get to see the 'highlights packages' of other people's lives and then compare them to their own. They feel like they are missing out on life and have no way to change their circumstances.

Playing sports matches can be an excellent way for them to learn to deal with nerves and anxiety. A more robust emotional system emerges and this can lead to social confidence. The nerves of a social situation that is out of our comfort zone can be compared to the feeling of apprehension before a sports competition. The ability to handle that feeling is a major key to enjoying life fully.

We can teach children to embrace feelings of anxiety as signs that they can grow from an experience. Sports people talk about 'butterflies in the stomach' as being a positive sign that they are ready to perform. Your child can learn to think this way and not to be crippled by the anxiety and fear of failing. If we let this anxiety prevent our children taking on challenges, they will be greatly restricted in their lives. Overcoming this anxiety helps build a strong confidence and determination in your child.

Cooperation & Collaboration

It's a very natural thing for young children to be selfish. We've all seen toddlers who don't want to share. This is something that needs to be gradually trained out of children, so they learn that they need to share and co-operate. Sport can be a great way for a person to learn the benefits of working together and producing a result by collaborating with others. By participating in sports activities and playing in teams, your child becomes part of a group as opposed to just being the main focus. By learning they are not the centre of the universe, your child can develop a much healthier attitude to relating with people.

It's natural for children these days to want attention and be tempted by the endless new pieces of technology and material items that are available to them and their friends. To counter the habit of thinking that happiness comes from owning the latest game or toy, as well as their tendency to want to 'fit in' or 'one up' other children, we can teach them how to play with other children and develop a healthy attitude towards others. Encouraging them to take an interest in other people and show appreciation for who they are reduces these kinds of self-serving behaviours. By focussing on physical activity, the game becomes more about including other people rather than simply beating them by having the best toy.

This is where sport can provide the crucial counter-balance to the difficulties that modern day parents have in controlling the influence of technology in young people's lives. When we don't feel the need to compete with others and try and out-do them with the possessions we own, people find it easier to relate with us. We can help others and contribute to something more than just our own interests. This is something technology can't teach our children.

Dealing With Conflict

We will encounter difficult people throughout our lives. Some people will be awkward to get on with, while others will try and stop us from being successful. It's best to learn about this reality early in life as opposed to trying to get through life avoiding it. Your child will be at a big disadvantage if they can't handle conflict in their adult lives: they themselves will either be difficult to deal with or be a victim of those who are more forceful.

It's a fact that life as a child is full of conflict. In the one- hour sessions I do in primary schools, I am constantly dealing with disagreements between children and stopping mini fights that break out. Even amongst friends, children of that age have problems learning to relate to each other. As adults, we sometimes can't say we're much better! No-one wants their child to suffer but we must ensure we don't go too far the other way. Wrapping them in cotton wool and not exposing them to necessary struggle will not serve them in the long run.

It's also true that children can be cruel. These days it's not uncommon for bullies to post videos online and make social media posts to get at their victims. If children take this online world too seriously, they are in real danger of developing anxiety issues with something that is totally out of their control. We all receive criticism of our actions and who we are. People with a strong sense of self-esteem can handle that and not be derailed by other people's attacks. Those who are less robust can be greatly affected by negativity and criticism. This makes them very ineffective in adult life as they are far too sensitive to thrive in social and work environments.

By competing in sporting events, your child will learn how to be resilient in the face of attacks from bullies. Bullying exists even in adult life and sport can again be an excellent way to deal with other people acting in an unreasonable or aggressive manner. Shelter your child all you like, but they will still have to deal with these situations at various times in their lives. I would suggest that the best thing you can do is to prepare them for that by developing the character traits to withstand criticism, conflict and bullying.

Remember: *prepare your child for the path, not the path for your child.*

We need to build into children an attitude of determination and an ability to prove people wrong, so that they are capable of dealing with all types of people. In the long run, people who get on well with others and handle conflict maturely will have a much easier road into adulthood. Having learnt how to compromise, they won't constantly be in disagreement with others and will have much healthier relationships.

Work Ethic

EXCELLENCE IS ABOUT STRIVING FOR WHAT IS JUST OUT OF REACH AND NOT QUITE MAKING IT; IT IS ABOUT GRAPPLING WITH TASKS BEYOND CURRENT LIMITATIONS AND FALLING SHORT AGAIN AND AGAIN. THE PARADOX OF EXCELLENCE IS THAT IT IS BUILT UPON THE FOUNDATIONS OF NECESSARY FAILURE.

MATTHEW SYED

Having a work ethic and working hard at things is not easy. We all struggle with it. It is like a muscle that is built in each of us, one we can continue to grow. As most of us know, accomplishing things and finishing what you start has a self-reinforcing effect. We feel more confident the next time we start a project or take up a new hobby. The danger for young people these days is that everything is so easily available; what training do they have to develop the 'work-ethic muscle'?

A work ethic – along with self-motivation – needs to be built gradually and naturally. It is very rare for a child to succeed without any internal motivation. Again, the key is balance – by pushing too hard, parents can extinguish the love and desire their child has to develop themselves. Also, parents need to avoid becoming the only source of motivation for their children. People like to use the example of Tiger Woods as an example of someone whose father pushed him to success. The reality, according to Woods, is that he was the one driven to improve, asking his father to train him. Motivation needs to be intrinsic, but as parents we can help nurture it.

One thing I see in young people is a tendency to quit very early in a challenge. 'It's too hard' or 'I can't do it' are phrases used by children who refuse to even try to beat the challenge. It's as if they want to see if it's possible and, usually after one attempt, they move on to doing something that is easier to accomplish. The idea of trying again is becoming less of an option in young people's minds.

To an extent, you want your child to have a bit of self-criticism. If they are totally happy with themselves and feel like they don't need to improve or have nothing to learn, they will never strive beyond mediocre results. We all know this is not a good mentality to have in any area of life – it leads to poor health and a lack of achievement.

Part of the problem here is patience. I regularly see young people attempting to learn a sport by jumping straight to the advanced skills before first mastering the basics. This impatience ends up with a lesser result. If you were to bake a cake, would you turn the heat up to the highest setting and fast forward the process? Or would you set it at the OPTIMAL temperature and let it cook in the proper amount of time? Your child's development is the same: the correct challenges need to be handled at the right time.

Patience is a skill that needs to be taught to young people, so they learn to enjoy the slow process of getting good at things. Some projects or skills take weeks, some months and others are processes that can take years. Without the patience to endure these periods – to be able to cope with the boredom of repetitive activities and early failures – how can we ever hope to stick at things that take time? We are all naturally impatient and want fast results, but to get good results we must learn to overcome that instinct and show some resolve.

Sport can be a great way to learn self-discipline and how to persist over the long-term. This can give children a solid foundation for later in life when they need to stick with things to achieve their goals. People often use sports phrases such as 'no pain, no gain', and for good reason. They are good lessons to carry forward into other areas of your life. One of the best payoffs is that your child's confidence rises when they focus on a skill and develop it. Seeing hard work and focus paying off encourages them to do more in the future.

Next, we look at how sport helps develop children's social skills.

4

HOW SPORT DEVELOPS SOCIAL SKILLS IN YOUNG PEOPLE

Arguably, the most important skills we can develop are our interpersonal abilities. Being able to communicate and socialise with people is important to all of our relationships in life, and will largely determine how well we will do in work settings.

While our interpersonal abilities are extremely important, social intelligence helps us in more ways than just 'getting on with people'. How we understand the world and interpret situations will be hugely affected by how developed our social skills are. Parents know how important it is that their child develops the ability to work together with people, make friends, and work in a team. These factors will affect their work life, close relationships and friendships throughout their lives.

But how do these skills develop? Can they be learnt while staring at a screen?

I believe sport can be a fantastic way for young people to learn a host of important social skills that will carry them forward into their adult lives. Team sport in particular develops the ability to work positively with other people, because team members have to put the group before individual interests. Without learning this, a young person can become difficult and selfish. With this ability, your child can develop into someone who gets on well with people and makes friends easily. For this reason alone, I recommend that you encourage your child if they show a keen interest in a team sport.

It is key that we instil in our young people an attitude of earning people's respect through conducting themselves properly and showing respect to others. No one is entitled to receive respect just because of who they are or regardless of how they behave. Respect comes from behaving in the right way. The culture around sport promotes this way of thinking – there is no fooling the scoreboard or your team-mates.

We now look in detail at the social skills that can be developed through sport. These include:

- Confidence, self-esteem and respect
- Teamwork
- Leadership
- The ability to handle conflict with people
- Humility & Likability
- The understanding of how to help others when they are down
- Making friends

Confidence

First on the list are confidence, self-esteem, and respect, all essential for becoming a healthy, well-functioning adult. It's difficult to imagine confidence without self-esteem, and neither will develop without respect for oneself and others. Developing these abilities is easier said than done, and is greatly influenced by how young people interact with their parents, families and teachers. Again, sport is an excellent training ground for learning these abilities and developing the confidence to socialise with others. Sitting in front of a *PlayStation* can never develop a child in the same way as time spent training with team-mates and sharing the challenge of competing and improving.

Sport can test a child's confidence and young people can be upset by sport. It does, however, develop a resilience that underpins the development of true confidence in the long-term. A person who is never tested in childhood will be a very fragile adult. Life inevitably tests all of us and it helps to have experienced some difficulty and know that you can come through if you persist.

Healthy children develop self-esteem and respect from real achievements, not from grandiose beliefs about being special because of who they are. Earning real respect is far more important than trying to force people to respect you through your confidence alone. People who simply *act* confident become very tiresome to be around, and this is where confidences becomes arrogance.

A serious issue these days is that more children than ever are pampered and spoiled. Spoiling a child also leads to adults with an exaggerated sense of their own importance, regardless of how accomplished they really are. This is an attitude that needs to be discouraged, otherwise we are setting up children up for major problems later. School teachers I speak to regularly highlight this trend in young people.

The long-term effects of spoiling a child do not show up in the teen years, but when they reach their 20s and 30s. We've all seen that person who can't put their own interests aside for the benefit of the group. Having never had to make any sacrifices or share their possessions as children, it doesn't make sense to them that, as adults, they need to take others into consideration. They seem to have one rule for themselves and a totally different set of standards for how others should treat them. Often these same people don't make the connection between their selfishness and the lack of quality people in their lives. As a result, they struggle to accomplish things and work together with others. Often they become frustrated that 'things just won't happen for them'.

In addition, your child needs to develop a confidence that is not reliant on you solving all of their problems for them. True self-esteem comes from self-reliance and knowing that you can look after yourself. When you smother your child too much, they never have the opportunity to learn how to take control over their own circumstances and solve problems without your support. Bit by bit, we must teach young people self-reliance and responsibility for their own lives.

Many times, I've seen children very anxious before their first day on one of our holiday camps. After they've settled in and made friends, the anxiety disappears. Parents who shelter children from opportunities to push through initial discomforts like these, are not allowing them to grow and develop a sense of independence. Sometimes, a parent can have a selfish desire to keep the child close to them.

Ultimately, it is healthy that your child eventually becomes completely self-reliant. You have to let them go gradually and expose them to challenges that will help them grow. By allowing them more self-reliance, they can fully become their own person. They will thank you for that understanding when they're older.

During teenage years, children need to reject the guidance of their parents to a certain extent. They want to form their own identity and they must be allowed to do this. Teenagers need to be able to find new role models so they are not entirely dependent on their parents to guide them. Having a bit of distance between you and your teen in the short-term is healthy as they develop self-reliance and independence. Children who grow up without a strong sense of self can become insecure adults. Without anything to tie their confidence to, their sense of self becomes very fragile and this can lead to depression and difficulties getting on with people.

Another consideration here is that teens sometimes struggle to find a purpose, and this is when they end up doing things they shouldn't be doing. When we have a purpose, we feel more secure. When we feel we are advancing and that the future will be even better than it is now, we wake up each day with enthusiasm for what we can do. This is a great perspective for a young person to have. With a sense of purpose, they are less prone to depression and self-doubt, complaints that are prevalent among young people these days. Sport can provide this healthy direction and focus.

We can't just cross our fingers and hope a young person will figure out how to be confident. They need a bit of direction to get them started. For an adult to have real confidence in who they are, they need some sense that they have achieved something in their lives. Finishing a few computer games, watching *YouTube* clips and *Netflix* shows won't give them this feeling of self-esteem and self-worth. For confidence to be strong and lasting, it needs to be robust and formed through experience. We can't be confident because we are told we should be. Confidence is something built on challenge and is tied to feeling that we can handle whatever life presents us with.

Teamwork

GOOD AGGRESSIVE PLAY ACTUALLY HELPS CHILDREN CONTROL THEIR AGGRESSIVE IMPULSES AND HELPS THEM DEAL WITH THE AGGRESSION THEY SEE AROUND THEM ON TV OR IN REAL LIFE.

LAWRENCE J. COHEN

Playing sports in a team shows your child the power of collective focus. They feel an added strength being in a team unit and gain energy from helping others. These are characteristics of a healthy adult that we should work to develop – these lessons will not be learnt automatically. At the same time, by contributing to a team's success and receiving congratulations from fellow players and coaches, children can build self-esteem and enjoy contributing and feeling connected to others.

I myself benefitted greatly from playing in sports teams growing up. Each new sports team I joined was different and provided a new set of social challenges. Playing with boys older than me, as well as men, allowed me to learn adult communication and social dynamics in a way that I wouldn't have been able to in a setting of children of my own age. This provided an excellent transition for me between my teen and adult years. Also, playing sport in other countries taught me how teamwork is seen differently in different cultures. Playing cricket in Australia showed me new perspectives on supporting teammates and standing up for each other that I hadn't seen in the UK, for example.

Some experiences can alter your attitude for good. Playing in just one good sports team can completely change a child's attitude to teamwork and teach them about group dynamics. These experiences are life-changing and can give children a new perspective on life. They also give young people the opportunity to create strong bonds of friendship and memories they can cherish later, providing key learning experiences for later in their lives.

A child who is not able to play in groups becomes very selfish. We must make sure young people understand early that it is in their own benefit to get on with people. If they don't understand this, they will continue to focus only on their self-interests and struggle to understand why everyone else seems reluctant to help them with their goals.

We often see this dynamic in our coaching sessions. A young child will feel he/she is superior to the others in the group. This attitude leads to disrespect of people around them and eventually the other children (and coaches) tire of this attitude. They become disconnected from the group but fail to see they are the problem, not everyone else. It's a very positive thing to see children getting on and working together. Often they will encourage each other when another player is upset and make real efforts to work together and sacrifice for the good of their team. Sport is such a great way for them to exercise these abilities and learn to get on with each other. They will make mistakes but they will certainly learn in the process.

Even simple games like hide-and-seek and tag teach key social skills and the ability to play in a healthy way. It's a shame that play like this is becoming a rarer form of entertainment. These games help children learn how to control their aggression and how to express it in a way that doesn't harm others. It's natural for young children to have conflict and even fight with each other. It's through these experiences that we learn what is right and wrong.

Team sports are also an excellent way to instil discipline in children. They need to learn to respect authority and to be a follower before they can develop leadership skills. Acting as if your child is destined to be a leader and never needs to follow any authority does a lot of damage to their interpersonal skills. They will feel others are beneath them simply because they are who they are. Other people don't respond well to this attitude. The people who get respect are the ones who show respect for others and who are prepared to support the team above their own self-interest.

As we will discuss next, you can't learn leadership abilities without an understanding of how a group operates and without the ability to get on with people effectively. These are essential lessons your child must learn on the path to becoming an effective adult.

Leadership

Leadership abilities are some of the most valuable skills an adult can have. There is no better way to introduce these dynamics to a young person than sport. Your child will learn to 'put the team first' and do things for the good of the group. These are character traits that make a person likeable. Selfish interest and ignoring the group are not positive ways to live as an adult.

One of the best training grounds for leadership is junior sports. Where else can your child have organised activity where he/she gets to exercise important attributes like motivating people, supporting those that are down, and managing group dynamics? Sport can be a trial-run of important scenarios that adults experience in their work and home life. By playing organised and structured games, your child can be tested in ways they might not otherwise experience.

Playing in sports teams also teaches your child leadership through the examples of their coaches and captains. By observing them, children can see what is good and what is negative. By gaining this understanding, they will have a better chance themselves if they need to fulfil leadership roles in other settings. By being exposed to different leadership styles, your child can learn which ones they resonate with. We all have different personalities and need to 'find our own voice'. Your child can learn to develop their own communication styles based on their strengths. By knowing themselves in this way, they'll be in a stronger position to thrive into adulthood.

I captained junior sports teams and it improved my confidence and ability to put myself forward in other areas of life. It's very important to understand that leadership skills can be developed. I certainly didn't always find it easy, particularly in my early teen years, but I was able to develop my leadership abilities with exposure and time. If your child ever aspires for responsibility at work or to start their own business, these skills can prove to be invaluable.

Humility & Likability

Sport is an excellent way for your child to learn to develop humility and likability. They will not always win their sporting contests and will have to learn to handle failure. Only through this process can a person develop true humility. A person who isn't tested at all may be able to maintain an arrogant front, but most people see through this behaviour for what it is: an act. Many parents make the mistake of encouraging an attitude of over-confidence in children, but this can lead to problems later. The real world is not tolerant of an over-inflated ego – people will expect real results. Not only does humility make a person more likeable (and popular), but it also grounds a person in reality and can allow them to see what they need to do to improve.

Learning empathy and consideration for others also makes a person likeable. No one wants friends who only think about themselves. To be a popular and likeable person, your child will need to be able to see things from other people's perspectives and get on with them.

A lack of interest in humbly taking advice is a worrying sign in a young person. You can't expect children to listen to every bit of advice you give them, but there should be signs they are open to listening and learning from someone. If your child sees others simply as tools to give them what they want, they will have problems later on. People sense an entitled attitude and are put off – they can't feel any warmth towards people who are out for their own benefit. Often these people don't realise why others don't want to be around them, and will find themselves with very few real friends. You can be confident and also still accept your limitations. This, in turn, makes you more likeable: people can connect and relate to who you are, and are at ease in your company.

Another downside of overconfidence is young people may feel they have nothing to learn, and that their life will always be good regardless of the effort the put in, leaving them with no determination to learn new skills. Having never struggled, they don't believe they ever will. My experience is that this path ends badly for young people. Overconfidence leads to a young adult who has a real lack of effectiveness, both in the workplace and socially.

Humour is another aspect of likability and is certainly something that can develop in sports teams. The changing room environments in sports have always been a place of playful humour and it is through these situations that a child can develop a sense of humour that is appreciated by others.

As much as you might hear otherwise, sport is not all about winning. We can learn excellent skills as a by-product of playing sport, and getting on with people is as valuable as any of them. Sport can be an excellent way for young people to learn how to respect others in competitive environments. By experiencing the challenges in group settings and team play, children discover the right and wrong ways to deal with people. This helps them build up positive ways of communicating so that other people want to be around them and help them. It's not a perfect process, but only experience can teach them these fundamental skills.

Friendship

All parents are concerned with their child's popularity and whether they have good friends. Sport can be an excellent way for children to bond and get to know each other with a mutual interest to focus on.

A lot of my friendships have been formed from playing in sports teams. By competing together, you form a strong connection with people and get to know each other really well. You have shared memories and joint accomplishments to enjoy with each other.

It's amazing how some sports activities and matches can create a connection between people. A shared struggle and accomplishment is remembered and often a friendship is built. There is a respect and appreciation between you that lasts. People often need an activity to connect with when they first meet someone. In the same way that we make friends at school by being in close proximity with certain people, sport brings people together and gives them a chance to forge friendships that otherwise wouldn't have happened.

Later in life, at university or in their work, your child can end up making friends due to mutual enjoyment of playing sport. Sports clubs are a fantastic way of building a social circle quickly in a new town, city, or country.

Travel

Another of the many benefits of your child playing sport are the many opportunities to travel. These days, even amateur sports teams travel to interesting places around the world. This provides your child an excellent chance to open their minds to new cultures, meet new people, and learn about the world.

Many of the children I coach are going on football trips to different parts of Europe, cricket tours to South Africa and Dubai, and rugby tours to New Zealand. I myself had the chance to live in Australia when I was 18 years old. I was able to make friends in Perth, Western Australia – I played a season of cricket there and worked as a sports coach to fund my trip.

Through playing cricket, I was able to make friends with people in many other countries. I was able to stay with friends in Australia, America, India and South Africa. Meeting people from different cultures also developed my social abilities so that I could make friends more easily when I was home.

The new perspectives gained from meeting people in these different cultures can really change how you look at your own life and give you a respect for people from different cultures. Traveling in sports teams is cheap and easy. I was able to stay with people from sports clubs and go to places I would never have been able to afford to visit without sporting contacts.

Travel like this is also a great way to encourage young people to expand out of their comfort zones. By being reluctant to leave a small circle of people and environments, your child may grow to fear circumstances they're not comfortable with. It's far better to gradually expose a child to new environments and get them used to a level of uncertainty. I personally remember feeling very uncertain as a child when I showed up at a sports club or holiday camp and I knew no one there. In hindsight, I'm glad I had those experiences. I am grateful I was able to push through those feelings so that they didn't stop me later in life. By desensitising myself to the anxiety of meeting new people, it became much easier later on.

In the next three chapters, we look at practical ways parents can encourage their child to be active, how to communicate effectively, and how to create a home that promotes physical activity.

5

HOW TO ENCOURAGE YOUR CHILD TO PLAY SPORT & BE ACTIVE

DEVELOPMENT IS ABOUT
THE APPROPRIATE CHALLENGE
AT THE RIGHT TIME.

Now that we've looked at the many positive benefits of sport for young people, the question is: How to encourage it? As a parent, you know that trying to force a child to do something is a battle you are likely to lose. We've all seen the resistance a child will put up when forced to do something. Also, being over serious and commanding your children to do what you feel is best doesn't help build affection or real connection between you.

Your job is to facilitate and enable your child to play sport. It's key that your children are motivated to play sport themselves, rather than doing it to please you. Sport should be something children are naturally drawn to. What's needed is a playful aspect to your relationship and sport can provide that.

How do we do this? We steer rather than direct. Give your children the opportunity to try different sports and activities so they can find something that resonates with their unique make-up. For one child it might be tennis, another volleyball. Exposing them to lots of activity gives them a chance to find something that really excites them.

If your child is not taking much interest in sport, it could be that they have not been exposed to a sport which captures them emotionally. If your child tried football but didn't enjoy it, don't give up. It may be that a bat and ball sport or athletics could be their thing. An excellent way to give your child a chance to try out different activities are multi-sport camps during the school holidays. I used to attend these as a child. Not only is your child able to try a variety of sports and learn what they like and dislike, they will also benefit by their bodies being challenged in different ways by the different activities.

This said, it's natural your children will reject your authority and want to be left alone at times. Allow for these phases of development but keep enabling sport in ways they are comfortable with, even if you're not involved that much. Each child is unique and will want to play at different intensities. It's for us to judge what our children are comfortable with and if it's best to slow things down or make them more challenging. Let them learn and discover at their own pace.

Understanding Your Child

How do we get to know the unique interests of our child? Two simple ways to do this is by noticing what they resonate with and giving them a chance to explore many different things. This gives children the support and attention they need to discover their passions in a natural way.

Oftentimes children lack confidence and this is where we can help build them up. By playing in a way they feel competent, children can build their confidence and enjoy physical activity. By keeping things playful and positive – getting them laughing and playing games – you can repair a child's damaged self-confidence,

If you sense your child is frustrated or tense, take them to the local park and play sport. This can be an ideal way to release the tensions that we often forget that young people feel. They have their own worries, as ridiculous as this may seem to us adults. Show them they can release this tension in a healthy way through playing and physically exercising.

If your child shows enthusiasm for a certain sport, encourage them. Find a club they can join, buy them the necessary equipment to play, find them some coaching so that they can enhance their love of playing and grow their abilities. The sport your child initially chooses may not be the one they settle on later. What's important is that your child learns to love moving, running, and hitting a ball or catching it. This is the first step in finding something they can stick with.

Once your child finds something they love to do, you won't need to push them to pursue it. This is a powerful thing. Instead of watching TV or playing the latest computer game, your child will want to go outside into the open air and release all the natural energy a young person has. Help them experiment and find that passion.

Also remember that children need different things at different stages of development. It's up to us to figure out what the appropriate challenge is. Ask them questions to help you discover what they are interested in, and pay attention to what your child says.

Being a Playful Parent

PLAYING WHAT THEY WANT TO PLAY, HOW THEY WANT TO PLAY IT, IS OUR WAY OF REALLY LISTENING.

LAWRENCE J. COHEN

You can enjoy the youthful energy of your children. They can reignite your imagination and teach you things. Enjoy playing with them and doing the activities that excite them. If they find some physical activity they enjoy – encourage it! And you can do more than just dropping your child at organised sporting activities, you can also play your own part by playing games and sport with them.

We communicate our own enthusiasm and energy levels when we play with our children. Don't just go through the motions. Your child will resonate with you far better if you try and meet them at their level and indulge their fun in whatever form it comes. Plus, the fact that you give them your full attention and are not distracted by your mobile phone is a big deal. Be prepared to leave your phone alone for a couple of hours and just focus on your child. They deserve it. By being patient and exploring what your child likes to do, together you may discover something they are really drawn to; this could lead to a new passion for your child that can last many years.

When I was very young, my father would take my younger brother and I to the park on Saturday afternoons. We would play 2 or 3 different sports for hours. We were able to dictate what we did and we loved this play time. You can do the same for your child: designate a day of the week or an afternoon when you take your child to the park or sports ground and play with them in whatever way they would like.

You can also invent games to play with your child in your house or outside. Instead of spending the night watching TV together, why not break things up with a game in the living room or back garden. It's tempting to be lazy as parents – but going through the motions and not making an effort to encourage physical activity in our children is not the right attitude. Get creative and allow them to explore playing games. *YouTube* is a great resource for finding examples of games to play.

You can use the time you play with your child to work on aspects of their character which might be lacking. For example, if you'd like to see more persistence from your child, help them to develop that by playing a game where they have to keep going even when they're tired. As with everything, we need to make this fun while showing them that there are rewards for showing the right attitude.

> PLAY, WITH ALL ITS EXUBERANCE AND DELIGHTED TOGETHERNESS, CAN EASE THE STRESS OF PARENTING. PLAYFUL PARENTING IS A WAY TO ENTER A CHILD'S WORLD, ON THE CHILD'S TERMS, IN ORDER TO FOSTER CLOSENESS, CONFIDENCE, AND CONNECTION. LAWRENCE J. COHEN

By teaching your child how to play in a healthy and considerate way, you're also teaching them how to connect with their friends. Always consider how your child will be in relation to others when you play with them. Bad habits tolerated at home can cause them problems elsewhere.

Another great benefit of play is that it's an excellent way for your child to release tension. In his excellent book, *Playful Parenting*, Laurence Cohen emphasises the importance of active play in a child's development. He talks of the therapeutic effect playing sport can have for a child who is stressed or experiencing the natural anxieties of being a young person. Like letting the air out of a balloon, the stress doesn't have a chance to accumulate if you are regularly allowing them a chance to let off steam. The physical exercise can release frustrations and make your child easier to deal with. Add this to the stronger connection you build by playing together, you will find your relationship with your child growing much stronger.

In all of this, we have to be prepared to play with our children in the way they want to play. It's not for us as adults to impose on children what they have to do all the time. We need to respect the phase of development our children are in and go with it, not against it. Challenge your child to sometimes be in charge but also to learn how to follow. Let them understand the benefit of both roles.

As parents, there's a delicate balance between following a child's lead and stepping in to help them – from building their confidence to challenging them to grow. We all have a need for connection and closeness with our children, it's something parents really value. By taking the initiative and at times following their lead, we can build connection with children through play. Keep inviting the child to connect, but offer to do it their way, on their terms. As a general rule, start out letting them win games, and then slowly play harder and harder so they are challenged. Teach them good sportsmanship and how to be competitive in a healthy and respectful way. We can reinforce that in the way we play with them from a young age.

With young children in particular, you need to let a lot go. Don't fight every fire that flares up in play – accept that there will be a certain amount of chaos with young children. Trying to create order out of what is naturally a chaotic situation will only frustrate you. We can't expect children to act like serious adults. Let them follow their own enthusiasm and steer them away from trouble if they're attempting to do something dangerous.

It can be hard work trying to get children to follow our lead. No one ever said being a parent is easy! But it is up to us to try and lead them into healthy mindsets towards physical activity that they enjoy. We must also make sure we are enabling them to play when they are enthusiastic, and even subtle things can make a big difference. By encouraging children when they want to watch sport, we can stir their imagination and let them find positive role models. Don't miss the opportunity to let them do this. Put your child first at times and allow them to get the correct learning experiences in each phase of their development.

> PLAY IS ONE OF THE BEST WAYS TO ENGAGE WITH CHILDREN, PULLING THEM OUT OF EMOTIONAL SHUTDOWN OR MISBEHAVIOR, TO A PLACE OF CONNECTION AND CONFIDENCE. LAWRENCE J. COHEN

Mistakes to Avoid

It's easy to point out the mistakes our children make, but we must also be aware we can make some ourselves. Most of us have heavy workloads and it's easy to become a distant parent, glued to our phones and distracted by the endless work admin we have.

We need to learn to know when it's time to put down our own digital devices and make our children our focus. Resist the temptation to hand over phones or other electronic devices to entertain children. Encourage them to play and find out what excites them in the real world.

Be positive about your children's play. It's easy to slip into the habit of being harsh with our children. Comments like 'good try' and 'nice catch' build confidence and trust. Any friction between you and your child will create an unpleasant atmosphere and they may be reluctant to try again.

Take care to give your children enough attention – and the right kind of attention. Driving children around and buying them things may seem like enough of an effort for a parent. Unfortunately, this often produces ungrateful and disconnected children who are very difficult to deal with, something I see all too often.

Put simply, the more we can play with our children in the right way, the more we can connect with them. A huge plus is we can then expect better behaviour generally, as there's a nice balance between fun and the desire we have for them to behave maturely. Although there will always be times when our children's activity is tedious for us, remember that children don't know how to adapt to adults, so be prepared to adapt to them and let them have their fun. They'll appreciate it later when they understand what you did for them. I can still remember playing with my Dad in the park and our back garden as he indulged me in my active imagination.

The Different Phases of Your Child's Physical Development

In my early years, I played football, rugby, ice hockey, tennis, table tennis, golf, pool and swimming before eventually deciding to put all my focus into playing cricket. Without doubt, this early 'sampling period' of trying different sports was essential in becoming physically active and being able to pick the one sport I loved.

This approach is backed by many scientific studies which suggest that sampling many different sports before the age of 12, then playing 2 or 3 in the early teens, and finally settling on a favourite at around aged 16, is the optimal way to learn sport. There are 'windows' to your child's physical development that must not be wasted. Once they're missed, developing proper co-ordination and strength can become extremely difficult.

Here are some suggestions for introducing your child to sports at different phases of their growth:

- **Aged 2–4.** This is the phase to introduce very simple movements to your child. Rolling a ball towards them and congratulating them when they stop it, is a great start. From there you can progress to dropping a soft ball into their hands and letting them enjoy playing games with you. Teach them to balance in a safe environment and go with the flow of their general enthusiasm for playing and running around. Buy some soft balls and bats to play with. The earlier your child starts developing their co-ordination, the better chance they will have of enjoying sport later. Let them play!

- **Aged 5–10.** Around this age, your child will become proficient in running, catching, and jumping if they've had adequate physical activity, although unfortunately this is not always the case these days. If your child shows interest in a sport, ENCOURAGE IT! Take them to sports camps and clubs. Buy them the equipment to play at home. Create obstacle courses in the garden to test their balance and co-ordination. Even if an activity is not your child's favourite thing as they get older, just the fact they have an enthusiasm for it is a great start in becoming an active person. If you let that opportunity go, they could fall into the technology trap and choose video games in their spare time. This is an excellent time to start children in holiday camps, too. Playing sport all day – and meeting new children in the process – is an excellent way of getting all the benefits discussed in previous chapters. Encourage them to try as many different sports as possible and continue to keep things fun.

• **Aged 10–13**. At this age, many children will have a sport they really enjoy. Often they will be playing 2 or 3 sports, although they may prefer one. Encourage your child to continue to play different sports. Playing different sports will really help develop rounded physical ability. In their mid to late teens, they can choose to specialise – but not yet. Again, school holiday camps and clubs can be a great way to get your child out of the house and doing something active. Encourage them to watch their favourite sports on TV too. They can then develop a real love of sport that will lead to them wanting to play more themselves. Take them to watch sporting events for the same reason. You are exciting their imagination and this is a very healthy thing.

• **13+.** During a child's teen years, they may develop a love for sport or prefer other things. Either is fine, obviously. Just ensure you're not doing anything to stop your child playing sport. Keep encouraging them if they want to join sports clubs and do some research yourself to find the best places. It's very healthy in their teen years that your child goes off to play sport without you. Accept that they want to develop their independence and let them do things the way they want to do them. Anything that prevents them playing sport at all is a bad idea, so don't be difficult with your children. Towards the mid-teen years, your child may decide that they have found their favourite sport. Continue to encourage this and support them however you can. Your child doesn't need to become the next global sports star. Playing sport consistently and to whatever level they desire, is exactly what you should encourage.

As I've mentioned, you have to let children go through the correct stages of their growth organically. Don't try and treat them like adults. Playfulness, not seriousness, should be the main focus. I've seen plenty of parents make the mistake of trying to 'train' their young children when playing sport. Let them play. The serious stuff can come from their sports coaches; with you they just want to have fun.

6

COMMUNICATING WITH YOUR CHILD EFFECTIVELY

THE MEANING OF A COMMUNICATION IS THE RESULT YOU GET.

RICHARD BANDLER

How do we communicate with children effectively, and what are the best methods for children of different age groups? While there are certain principles we can all abide by, communication is far more of an art than a science. Each child has his/her own particular personality and temperament, so a one-size-fits-all approach is never going to work. This chapter offers some guidelines for how sport can help you with your job as a parent.

My experience as a sports coach has taught me certain methods that are effective in steering children in the right direction. The way we speak with young children is very important. The tone and energy behind how we communicate can completely change the meaning of our words. What's great about sport is that it can provide us with a context to teach important lessons to young people.

General Tips for Communicating With Your Child

- A 'head masterly' tone is not often effective; we need to be versatile enough to know the right approach at the right time.
- Laughter is a great tension reliever. As discussed in the section on 'Playful Parenting', you should be laughing a lot with your child. If you're on edge, they will be on edge and will distance themselves, leaving you to struggle to get them to follow your lead. Connect through good humour and let them release tension when they're around you.
- Be consistent with the messages you give young children. For them to understand what good behaviour is, they need to have that consistently shown and trained into them. Your children will model a lot of their behaviour and communication on what they experience at home.
- Help children through disappointments. Things don't always go their way, and it's inevitable that your child will make mistakes. Teach them how to handle disappointments and move forward by discussing with them how to interpret events correctly.
- Lead your child from a place of fear to a place of real confidence. As a parent, you are creating the self talk

> that is in their heads. Teach them a positive outlook and train them to think optimistic thoughts about what they're trying to do. We need to make sure we do this in an empowering way. Something that works really well with children is to highlight and exaggerate when they do something well and with a good attitude. You can often see them light up and grow in confidence from this praise.

Our job as parents, teachers and coaches is to guide children so that they develop into well-functioning adults, and that rests on the quality of support and encouragement we provide them. We start with perhaps the most crucial framework for any child: *the Growth Mindset.*

The Growth Mindset

In a growth mindset, people believe that their most basic abilities can be developed through dedication and hard work—brains and talent are just the starting point. This view creates a love of learning and a resilience that is essential for great accomplishment. Carol S. Dweck

A concept that has become popular recently is the idea of 'The Growth Mindset'. If there is one important idea to instil in young people, it is the idea that ***your life will improve if you work hard***. Without this mentality, young people can fall into bad habits and develop negative beliefs about the world.

A positive mindset and healthy attitude to hard work is also a key ingredient in a person's confidence. With it, they feel they are in control of their lives. Essentially, we can have one of two mindsets:

1. We believe our talents and abilities are fixed and beyond our control to change.
2. We believe we have control over our development and can improve through hard work and dedication.

It is the second mindset that we want to teach to our young people to ensure they grow into effective adults.

People without a growth mindset tend to think things are outside of their control. They are unable to take destiny into their own hands. Without the belief that they can achieve, they never try. They often don't feel they have any weaknesses that can be improved on. This denial leads to playing things very safe and never trying to achieve anything. Alternatively, without a belief that we can change our circumstances, why would we try? It's very damaging for a young person to believe that they are simply 'not good at something' and there is no point continuing because they can't get better.

Encouraging behaviours of persistence and effort are vital. It's very effective when parents, teachers and coaches subtly reinforce the growth mindset in young people. If your child achieves a result through hard work, make sure to praise them and reward them. If they work hard and don't receive the reward, continue to encourage them and remind them that they will get their reward sooner or later. I'm sure you can see how sport can be a natural way to encourage this mindset.

Comments such as 'well done, you deserve that for working so hard' are very important. Connecting success and hard work is one of the most important lessons a young person can learn and it's often lost in the modern approach of being softer with children. In honest attempts to look after their children, parents can often teach them unhelpful mindsets that will confuse them later. Rewarding a child when their effort has been poor can lead to an entitled and incapable character.

The right amount of praise must focus on the quality of praise rather than the quantity. It should be genuine and appreciative of the effort that the child exerted and not on the actual result. The outcome is just a bonus. Robin Murphy

A good mindset to instil is that 'you get what you deserve'. While real life isn't quite a simple as that, it's a good mentality for young people. Remember, children can't understand the subtleties of life yet and they need simple beliefs to follow. By encouraging them to earn what they get, they will learn to take charge and work towards what they want.

A child who receives constant criticisms or being compared to other children and made to feel inferior will stop trying and withdraw to prevent being noticed. He feels it is safer and better to pull away since he does not belong and is not perfect. Rebecca Eanes

The worst thing you can do is encourage a mentality that there is no point in trying. I sometimes see this pessimistic attitude in parents and it can be really toxic for a child. As a parent, you must err on the side of being positive and enthusiastic for what is possible for your child. Children pick up on this and it becomes a self-fulfilling situation. Beliefs leads to effort and effort leads to results.

If you expect things to not go well, they often do. This is a terrible mindset for young people to learn, and the opposite of what we should encourage. We need to reinforce both a POSITIVE and OPTIMISTIC mentality in our young people. These are the best mindsets to achieve success and happiness. It becomes an upward spiral where success leads to more belief and more enjoyment of life. This approach also makes people want to be around us.

By providing a stable but balanced home environment, you give your child the best chance to develop a grow into a well-functioning adult. The judgement from you needs to be: *when am I being too hard, and when am I being too soft?* Young children are like sponges, absorbing your views, outlook and behaviours. Keep your own attitude positive and optimistic around your children. This will rub off on them in a powerful way. You are shaping how they think about the world. For instance, parents who are overprotective will shape their kids to fear going out of their comfort zone. Being fearful yourself will rub off on your child.

> No one slides through childhood without some feelings of frustration, helplessness, and powerlessness. When powerlessness rears its ugly head—and it inevitably will—Playful Parenting can help children back to confidence and competence. Lawrence J. Cohen

Again, communication is an art so these are just general guidelines to consider and by no means are concrete directions about what to do in all circumstances. What motivates your child may not be what motivates another. Some children like to play sport for the pure fun of it and others want to use sport as a way to challenge themselves. Often well-intentioned parents will make every effort to help their child, but be working against the natural way that young people learn and are motivated to do things.

Drop any judgement of your child and allow you and them to discover who they are. Don't try and mould them, but let them take shape naturally. In fact, trying to mould them often leads to them rebelling in the opposite direction.

Sport and the Growth Mindset

That is the thing about purposeful practice: it is transformative. And that is true whether you're into table tennis, tennis, football, basketball, typing, medicine, mathematics, music, journalism, public speaking – you name it.

Matthew Syed

Sport is arguably the best way to teach children a growth mindset. The nature of playing sport encourage participants to work on the different skills required to get better results. With this mentality, your child can go on to achieve other things in their lives. A positive mentality opens up our minds to new possibilities. We are excited by challenge and confident we can have a positive outcome in trying new things. We feel we are in control of our lives and circumstances. It's also very clear that a positive mindset leads to better physical health. Our bodies begin to reflect the positivity of our thinking. People want to be around those who have a positive approach and drive to move forward. These types of people have a magnetic energy that draws people to them. They feel that their life will be better around this person.

In addition, young people often find role models and heroes from watching sport. They aspire to be like the sportspeople they see on television and this motivates them to achieve in their own lives. If they find positive role models in sport, encourage them. Buy them posters and books so they can learn more. Young people need other humans to copy. Social media and online celebrities will not benefit them in this regard.

Sport can provide experiences for these children that show them that they can overcome initial difficulty. This is essential for their future success. This process can also train your child to enjoy the act of practicing to get good at things. Again, this makes them far more likely to be successful in whatever they try later in life.

In particular, sensitivity to difficulty and criticism leads to increased stress and anxiety. Everything becomes amplified and the effects can stop people progressing past a certain point. We need to learn to endure the tedious nature of repetitive practice to be good at anything. We develop the ability to focus deeply and enjoy the short-term pain that leads to a long-term pay off.

This idea that there is nothing more common than a talented person who squandered opportunity is certainly true from my experience. It's also an excellent lesson to teach young people. I often hear children talk about how good another child is at a sport or some other talent that they have. It's crucial that we instil in children that they are not fated to finish behind people simply because they might not have the same natural abilities. Encourage them to keep striving and tell them that they can go even further than their talented peers if they work harder. This is certainly true and a very positive belief to have.

Communicating With Young Children

It's far easier to get things right with a child from day one, than to try and make up for mistakes later on. We've all been around children who were mishandled at a young age and are troublesome as a consequence. As a parent, you are helping yourself as much as anyone by instilling the correct discipline and values early on so that you don't have to make big corrections in the difficult teen years. Having said this, discipline must be balanced with affection and playfulness in young children. An overly serious and disciplined approach can cause the opposite response: a child who causes you difficulties because of the frustrations and tension you are causing.

Praise nurtures your kid's sense of self, self-esteem, and confidence. This is the reason why you need to verbalize your appreciation when you like his behaviour as soon as you catch him. Rebecca Eanes

When dealing with children in their formative years, we need to have a playful and positive approach. We are building the model of how the child see's the world. At this stage of their development, children don't need a tough approach. We don't need to build a serious and mature person now – that can come later. We have to forgive some bad behaviour and steer children toward good behaviour rather than expecting perfection right away. They need to connect with you so that they can respond to your guidance. That requires you to adapt.

It's very important that we praise young children when they behave or play well. We can't assume they will know they did the right thing or that they know you are proud of them. Tell them they've done well and ensure they feel good about playing in a positive way. This approach reinforces good behaviour and creates more of it, something I've seen many times.

Discipline is important in the development of any child but it is particularly difficult in young children. If you over use the strong approach, you can lose your effectiveness in trying to create good behaviour. You have to learn to 'pick your battles' and know when you can let certain bad behaviours go. Trying to manage all acts of bad behaviour in a young child is tiring and unproductive. Pick the important moments and let kids be kids.

Sometimes children are acting up simply to get your attention. This can be a sign that we need to connect with them and play with them instead of trying to police the activity and discourage bad behaviour. Sport can be a great way of developing that connection and steering them to positive behaviours.

Young children are prone to tantrums over what we see as very insignificant issues. It's important not to reward that behaviour. Sometimes, we have to let them have their moment without trying to appease them. Often a tantrum is just a child's need to release tension and frustration. Again, sport can be a good release for a child and the tantrums will be far fewer when you have a child who is exhausted from a full day playing sport, I can promise you that!

With the correct communication, we can teach children healthy attitudes towards competing with other children. We must reinforce the idea that winning is not everything. It's natural that some children will be extremely competitive and want to dominate other children at times but we should again try and steer them towards a more considerate approach to playing with other children. Teach them this when you play together:

encourage them to treat you fairly and they will behave the same way with other children.

Spend time playing positively with your child early on, and you will be rewarded with a young person who feels connected to you and has a foundation for good behaviour. If you miss the opportunity to do this from the start, your job will be doubly difficult later on as you try and reverse bad behaviours that could have been prevented from forming in the first place.

Communicating With Teenagers

IT IS A HEALTHY PART OF YOUR DEVELOPMENT TO FOLLOW A PATH INDEPENDENT OF YOUR PARENTS AND TO ESTABLISH YOUR OWN IDENTITY.

ROBERT GREENE, *MASTERY*

IF YOU'RE GOING TO BE INDEPENDENT AT 22 YOU MAY NEED TO START RATTLING THE BARS OF THE CAGE AT 14.

NICOLA MORGAN

It's hard being a teenager. We often forget this as adults. From our point of view, teenagers have an easy life without the stresses and responsibility of being an adult.

It's important to remember that teenagers deal with a lot of frustration and doubt. Their arrogance and cockiness is often a front for a lot of tension and worry about who they are and who they are becoming. Teenagers are naturally very unsure of where they fit in and who they are. They are yet to discover these things so there will naturally be a lot of tension within them.

In my first few years of coaching teenagers, I was often very frustrated with the disobedience of teenagers. I just saw them as having bad attitude. My opinion has changed. I now see a young person who is in a transition between being a child and learning independence. It is this understanding which explains a lot of the bad behaviours we experience with this age group.

Teenagers are very emotional due to the hormonal changes that are taking place. We have to expect volatility and be patient as they learn to behave properly. Part of this process is your child feeling like 'they don't need adults to tell them anything.' Teenagers feel like they know what they need to do. This is a natural phase of their development and it's best to smile and let them go through it. It's common for teenagers to experience bouts of low self-esteem as they feel 'things aren't working out' for them. As a parent you can certainly help with these periods, but at times they will want to go it alone.

Another important factor to recognise is that teenagers need a lot of sleep! Parents often mention to me that they feel their child is lazy and sleeps too much. I try to reassure them that sleeping a lot is natural for a teenager. They are growing fast physically and also their brains are changing. They need their rest, so it can be counter-productive to hassle and argue with a very tired teenager. Scientists estimate that teenagers need 9 ½ hours sleep a night! Let them have their lie ins and they will grow naturally into their bodies; they will be easier to deal when they get the full rest they need.

Teenagers often have a real need for excitement in their lives. This is another reason I feel so strongly that sport can be a very healthy way to spend their time. We all know that teenagers can get up to trouble and do things they shouldn't. Without the excitement and fun in their lives that they crave, they will be far more likely to chase negative activities and influences.

Difficult Teenagers

I once asked a 73 year old great grandmother who had had a hand in raising dozens of children what she would recommend for effectively communicating with teenagers. She took a long breath, sighed, and said 'Huw, it's very difficult'.

We all know from experience that teenagers can be totally irrational at times. A child can go from a sweet and pleasant member of the family to a difficult monster almost overnight. Understandably, many parents find this quite hard to take. The hormonal changes and growth that are taking place mean that we can only hope to try our best to influence someone who is now set on making their own way and developing independence.

As a sports coach, it can be a similar story. Whilst primary school children can be boisterous and difficult to control, you don't get the disrespect and dismissive attitude of a badly behaved teenager.

Communicating Effectively With Teens

Now we get to the difficult bit. How do we communicate with teenagers who are resistant to our influence?

I think the first principle to remember when dealing with teenagers is to stay calm. Much easier said than done, of course, but by becoming irritated and bickering with teenagers, we promote more disagreement. Sometimes we need to let them release their tension and frustration and move on without making the conflict worse.

Taking the disrespect you get from teenagers is hard. It's natural to be frustrated and angry with how irrational they are. Learn to forgive them and recognise the big changes taking place in their brains and bodies. By becoming upset and angry yourself, you are teaching your child to argue with you. It's far better to teach them to keep their composure and deal with disagreements maturely. We can only do that by setting the example ourselves. This is why commanding teenagers to get off their electronic devices is so frustrating.

I've often see a parent squabbling with their teenage child. I feel that no progress can be made that way. We do need to enforce discipline when really necessary, but don't be constantly fighting with your teenager. You will lose your influence over them completely that way. As much as you might be frustrated by the way your teenager speaks to you or behaves around the house, you must find a way to keep things positive between you. Forgive them a bad day or even a bad week, and go back to positive communication between you.

Encouraging Your Teenager to Play Sport

Although children generally become more independent in their teens years, you as a parent still have a lot of influence and can help guide your child in the right direction. When it comes to sport, your job now is to facilitate and guide your child in the directions in which they show interest. At times, it may feel you have become a glorified taxi driver, but this is essential work for you as a parent. Much as they will be reluctant to admit it, they need you to create opportunities for them to pursue their sporting passions.

As I mentioned in the previous section, sport is an excellent way to keep your child away from trouble and negative temptations. Without some sort of focus they will go astray. The great thing about sport is that you can leave your difficult teenager in a safe and controlled environment. They can let off steam there in a healthy way instead of bottling it up and taking it out on you and your family. Again, don't *tell them* what to do, go with their enthusiasm.

If your child asks you to take them to a sports club, find a way to make that happen. Even if your child shares a lift with another child in order to get there, you need to do all you can to enable the activity. Relations between you and your child will be far better if they can see you are trying to help them follow their passions. Let them know you are trying your best to help them. If they doubt that, it will deeply hurt them.

You may find your teenager is happy for you to just drop them off at their sports practices and they don't want you to stay. This is perfectly natural. Often teenagers feel distracted if their parents are watching their every move. Part of their enjoyment is being free and doing an activity independently. Allow them to do this, even if you would like to stay and watch them play. By staying, you may make them uncomfortable and lessen their enjoyment of sport.

8 Mistakes to Avoid as a Sporting Parent

In my 15 years as a sports coach, I have not just dealt with a lot of children, I have also got to know their parents and observed the different approaches people take to bringing up children.

While nearly every parent has good intentions, we often see communication that is very counter-productive to the results intended. Here I have listed 8 common mistakes I see parents making when attempting to influence their children:

1. **The Helicopter Parent.** It's natural to want to be there for your child and it is essential a child feels supported. However, The Helicopter Parent takes this too far. The name comes from the idea of a helicopter constantly circling around a child to keep a constant eye on their activities. Whilst the intention is good, this is harmful to children if taken too far. There is a time to leave your child alone and let them develop some self-reliance. A habit I see in a lot of parents these days is that they take a lot of photos and videos of their child when they're playing sport. I've had parents walking into the middle of our sports sessions to take footage. If you want to take a picture or short video clip, that's fine, but don't distract your child or make them feel self-conscious. Know when it's time to step away and leave them to it.
2. **The Perfectionist Parent.** Some parents take their desire for the best life possible for their child too far. They demand unrealistic standards of children and this can do damage to their motivation. By demanding too much and criticising mistakes, they develop a fearful and frustrated mindset in children. Often this can lead to a child giving up or rebelling against the pressure. Training your child to be a perfectionist can cause them a lot of frustration and fear. The self-talk that is impossible to please can be lasting and cause your child to lose enthusiasm for what they're doing. Often this is said to come from a parent who feels they should have achieved more themselves.
3. **The Impatient Parent.** Often a consequence of expecting adult thinking from children, parents can become impatient that their child won't do what they

say. Remember: work ethic is like any of characteristic. It must be DEVELOPED. Don't expect it to be there straight away. Just nudge your child along instead of trying to fast track them to the end point. Let time do its thing and your child will mature naturally and effectively.

4. **The Overly Soft Parent.** It's a reality that your child will face difficulty or conflict at some point. This is the way of the world and we can do more harm than good by sheltering children from experiencing this a bit. All children need emotional support but smothering a child with too much sympathy and not allowing them to develop resilience is not preparing them adequately for adult life. A balance needs to be struck and that is going to be unique to your child and the relationship you have with them.
5. **The Worrier Parent.** There will always be anxiety and worry about your child's well-being and happiness. Take care not to transfer your anxious and overly fearful mentality onto your child. Parents can sometimes stifle their child's enthusiasm by focussing too much on what could go wrong. This fearful mentality could stop your child being open to trying new things or stepping into situations when they are feeling nervous. As a parent, you need to be aware of the language you're using with your child. Your criticism will become their self-talk, even in adulthood. This approach can also have the opposite effect, where they take dangerous risks.
6. **The Coach Criticiser Parent**. Some parents refuse to admit their child is wrong or that they misbehave. All children misbehave, and looking after groups of children can be a very challenging task. Be

careful not to take the side of your child too much, or side with them when they are behaving poorly. You will reinforce the bad behaviour and this will harm them in the long run. Ensure you can look at your child objectively and you will be able to reinforce the correct behaviours that will lead to them being a well-functioning adult. Don't speak negatively of sports coaches or teachers in front of your child. I was working at a school once where the parents got together to have the rugby coach sacked of a team of underperforming 12-year olds. The sports teachers were aware that the group were a small team that would naturally struggle in a very physical game. The parents, however, chose to place the blame on the coach. We all thought this to be a terrible message to be sending their children.

7. **The Best Friend Parent**. it's very important your child develops a sense of independence and is not totally reliant on you. It's natural to want to be involved in what your child is doing and to an extent, you should. However, be careful not to get in the way of your child forming friendships independent of you. Let them play with other children with you at a distance. You don't need to manage all of their relationships. Let them learn lessons of friendship, conflict and dealing with a bit of anxiety without you. As long as these situations are not too harsh, they will help develop your child into someone with a strength of character and social confidence.
8. **The Overly Serious Parent.** Keep a playful and positive dynamic with your child. If things are overly serious, your child will begin to resent you and rebel against what you want. Let your children play and be

> themselves. We can't expect adult maturity from children, so let them get away with being a bit silly and immature. Again, there is a balance to be struck, but you can be too hard and disciplined with a child. I saw a case recently of parent getting it wrong with his 14 year old. The father harshly berated his son for a lack of effort when playing cricket together. The father walked away from his son, who was on the verge of tears at the coldness of his father. It was difficult to see how the father could justify such an approach, but this type of communication upsets and demoralises children. Your child is not your 'achievement project' that you can use to put right your own frustrations. Let them learn and grow in a positive way that they enjoy.

Next, we'll discuss how to set-up a home environment that is conducive to your child being physically active.

7

CREATING A HOME ENVIRONMENT THAT PROMOTES PHYSICAL ACTIVITY

Psychologists like to discuss the idea of 'nature vs nurture', which essentially is the idea that we are a product of both our genetics and our environment. Based on my own experience and many discussions with others, I firmly believe that your home environment plays a huge role in how your children will develop.

I used to spend almost every possible moment playing sport – in the back garden, at the local park, and even in the living room with my brother. I feel very strongly that all that time added up to a love of and ability to play sport that helped me greatly as I grew into my teen years and adulthood. Friends re-iterate the same experiences. These days, I regularly speak to parents who are concerned that their children aren't getting the active childhood they had due to fears of them going outside.

It's understandable that parents are fearful of letting their children go outside alone, due to horror stories of un-thinkable things happening to children over the last 20 to 30 years. One parent recently described to me his fear of the rise in London knife crime, which made him very reluctant to allow his child to travel to school on the bus. What we need to do is come up with a solution to ensure our children are not sitting inside and missing out on the physical development and outdoor play that we had.

My suggestion is to get creative. What games can you allow your children to play in your home? What could you buy for them that will encourage them to play and develop a love of physical activity? As a parent, you must engage with your child and show them how to play. Go with their enthusiasm and encourage them to get on their feet and move. Invent games to play together in the lounge or back garden. Create spaces in your house where they can do this. Too often parents want to bring up children in 'show-home' type environments. Kids must be allowed to roam and move around. Remember, we are trying to get them to be active instead of passive. Is it fair for us to restrict the space our child can play in for the benefit of having a nice looking home? Is it not far more important your child has the freedom and opportunity to play?.

We also need to lighten up and create a playful atmosphere. Fun and laughter are what's needed to encourage young children and we need the right environment to promote that. We can't be too precious about our homes. It's the children who should be at the top of our list of priorities.

By playing with children at home, you can expect better engagement and, consequently, better behaviour. I've seen this with friends of mine who have a healthy playfulness in their relationship with their children. More often than not, the most difficult children come from stiff and serious households.

Ways Your Child Can Learn Sport

Children learn sport in a variety of different ways. It's not just about the organised sessions that schools or clubs put on for them. Ideally, your child will spend most of their free time playing and exercising.

One way you can encourage your child to spend more time outside playing is to find time to take your child to the local park or sports grounds. As I mentioned previously, if you have an afternoon free on a Saturday, suggest to your child that you go out and play. Another way is to find half an hour in the evening after work to play in the back garden with your child. All of these short periods add up to something significant if you do them regularly. Your child will thank you later for the time you spend with them.

This type of thing used to be commonplace but has become far less frequent among parents. As parents, it's not our job to simply drive our kids around and drop them off at activities. We should play an active role in how they develop and playing with them at the park or the back garden is as good a way as any.

Once the school term is finished, enrol them in a holiday camp. These provide excellent opportunities for your child to spend a full day outside in the sun, playing sport and meeting other children. I have worked at children's holiday camps for 15 years and have seen the huge benefit to children's growth and development. Often a child will come to every day of our 7 week holiday camps and make friends as well as improve their sporting abilities. As a parent, gently and lovingly push them to continue and let them work through the nerves of going into a new environment. Remember, the ability to meet new people and deal with nerves will be a key part of their adult lives, so building confidence in this way can be invaluable.

Ideas for Your Home

It's important that we set up a home environment to encourage our children to physically play. This means creating space for them to move around and objects for them to play with. Without space for kids to create and invent games, they will resort to the very problems and bad habits discussed earlier. Naturally they will want to find the most entertaining thing in their immediate environment. We should make this physical play. The hours spent playing at home build a love of play that will carry over into school sports activities and later into adulthood.

There are many items you can leave around your house to encourage your child to play sport. Some of the best ones in my experience include:

- Soft balls and bats for inside the house
- A table tennis table (this can be used inside and folds up for storage)
- Inflatable balance disks (to develop balance and body co-ordination in a fun way)
- Trampolines
- Indoor soccer goals to be used with foam balls or outdoor goals for your back garden
- Tennis balls and other sports balls in the garden
- A small tennis net in the back garden
- A kids basketball net for your back garden
- Indoor and outdoor jungle gyms
- Inflatable boxing stations for kids to play fight
- Mini hurdles and footwork ladders to invent obstacle courses

If you live in a wet climate, something that you might consider is replacing some of the grass in your garden with a soft artificial surface such as 4G AstroTurf. This allows children to go out and play when the rain stops. An exterior light attached to the house can also allow them to stay out and play longer. Every little thing you do to encourage your child to play physically can make a big difference to the decisions they make.

The real key here is to set up space. If you have a large coffee table in the middle of your lounge, consider removing it. It's far better to have a large space in the middle of your room where your child can invent their own games and play with their friends and siblings. Too often I see a parent's home that is decorated and furnished as if it is a show home. Perhaps consider if it's right for you to have expensive ornaments on display at this phase of your child's development. This is not taking into consideration the experience of your child and will greatly limit their development. Even one hour of play a day is 365 hours a year. Don't restrict your child by having an unhelpful home environment.

I grew up with a small back garden in London that was about 20 yards long and 7 or 8 feet wide. The limited space didn't stop my brother and I from playing hours of football, tennis, table tennis, cricket, rugby and whatever other games we took an interest in. These games even carried on inside when the light went down or the weather became too harsh in the English winter. We played games in the lounge and even had the table tennis table inside for a while. I taught myself to catch in our back room using the sofa cushions to protect me from a hard fall as I would dive across the room to catch tennis balls I'd thrown against the wall. I have to thank my mother for her patience and acceptance that her two boys wanted to play. Her beloved garden took quite a hammering but it was a youth well spent and children were always around our house to play with us.

Just recently, a friend was telling me he would like to see his eight-year-old son playing more instead of spending so long inside playing computer games. He and his partner had bought him a darts board in the hope that he would play that instead. When the boy showed me the board, I realised he had no idea how to play by himself, so had not yet tried. I showed him a few games and he was instantly engaged. Later I played outside with him in his driveway using just a tennis ball and whatever we could find. He was catching and throwing and we created games where I could challenge him. The joy he showed was very interesting. From a child who couldn't be taken away from his television screen, we had a boy who was jumping up and down, arms in the air and smiling ear to ear. He couldn't have been happier.

The time you spend with you children playing games and sport, taking them to sports clubs and activities they really enjoy, are worth it – both in the moment and long term. You are setting the foundation for their development in so many ways that will benefit them in their adult lives. Try your best to ensure their home environment is set up in a way that allows them to have fun and play!

CONCLUDING THOUGHTS

By reading this book, you've shown you care about your child's development. Not all parents are open to reading a book that might shine a light on how they can improve as a parent. This has been my attempt at illustrating the many benefits of playing youth sports in both an organised and unstructured way.

We don't yet know the long-term effects that the influx of technology will have on society as a whole. Parenting has always been challenging but the circumstances in which our children are growing up have changed drastically over the last 20 years. We must learn to manage these changes and not allow them to rule our lives and dominate our children's developmental years completely.

We must also use solid principles of child psychology and physical development to ensure our young people get the correct environmental influences. We can't experiment with their development. You wouldn't deprive your child of the opportunity to learn basic maths, so why should you accept a poor physical education?

I hope this book has given you an understanding of how sport can play a role in your child's overall development, not just in their physical health but also in their ability to handle challenges in their lives. Children need physical activity. They don't need to be training for triathlons, but they do need to be testing and developing their bodies as they grow.

Left to their own devices (no pun intended), our children are at risk of becoming dysfunctional. Alternatively, if we can find a balance of active and passive play, we can achieve the result of a healthy, happy and well-adjusted child. It's essential we teach them that sport can be fun and find creative ways for the conditions to be in place for them to play – they don't get to make it up later.

It's my hope that your child can live a balanced, happy and healthy life. This book has been my attempt to help you with that. I hope it has given you new perspectives and ideas that you can use in the unique way your child will respond. As I mentioned in the Introduction, there's not just one way to do things. We must be creative and responsive to the little human being in front of us.

To summarise the philosophies of this book:

- Provide the conditions and environment for your child to play
- Encourage them playfully and positively
- Let them learn naturally at their own speed.
- Focus on enjoyment.

I wish you all the best in the journey of bringing up your child and thank you for reading.

Huw Jones
May 2020

BIBLIOGRAPHY

Books

Babylonian Clay Tablet, in Greene, Robert, *The Laws of Human Nature*, Profile Books 2018.

Carr, Nicholas. *The Shallows: How The Internet Is Changing The Way We Think, Read and Remember*. Atlantic Books 2011.

Cohen, Lawrence J. *Playful Parenting: An Exciting New Approach To Raising Children That Will Nurture Close Connections*. Ballentine Books 2012.

Dweck, Carol S. *Mindset: The New Psychology of Success*. Ballantine Books 2007.

Eanes, Rebecca. *Positive Parenting*. J.P. Tarcher US Publishing 2016.

Greene, Robert. *Mastery*. Profile Books 2012.

Greene, Robert. *The Laws of Human Nature*. Profile Books 2018.

Mayer, David, and Keith Mayer. *Gold Dust: How To Become A More Effective Coach*. Independently Published 2019.

Morgan, Nicola. *Blame My Brain: The Amazing Teenage Brain Revealed*. Walker Publishing 2013.

Murphy, Robin. *Positive Parenting: How To Raise Sound Children and Be An Amazing Parent*. Amazon EU 2019.

Syed, Matthew. *Bounce: The Myth of Talent and The Power Of Practice*. Fourth Estate (GB) 2010.

Studies

Anderson, Jenny. 'Nearly 30% of teens sleep with their phones, but parents' device use may be more problematic'. *Quartz* (29 May 2019), at https://qz.com/1629889/survey-kids-increasingly-concerned-about-parents-device-addiction/.

Berger, Itai, et al. 'Brain Development and The Attention Spectrum'. *Frontiers in Human Neuroscience* (5 February 2015), at https://doi.org/10.3389/fnhum.2015.00023.

Bhat, Jyothsna. 'Attention Spans In The Age Of Technology'. *National Alliance on mental Illness (NAMI)* (14 August 2017), at https://www.nami.org/Blogs/NAMI-Blog/August-2017/Attention-Spans-in-the-Age-of-Technology .

Keles, Betul, et al. 'A Systematic Review: The Influence Of Social Media On Depression, Anxiety and Psychological Distress In Adolescents'. *International Journal of Adolescence and Youth* 25, no.1 (2020), at https://doi.org/10.1080/02673843.2019.1590851.

Knell, Gregory, et al. 'Prevalence and Likelihood of Meeting Sleep, Physical Activity, and Screen-Time Guidelines Among US Youth'. *JAMA Pediatrics* (2019), at https://jamanetwork.com/journals/jamapediatrics/article-abstract/2723518.

Lenhart, Amanda. 'Teens'. *Pew Research Center* (9 April 2015), at https://www.pewresearch.org/internet/2015/04/09/teens-social-media-technology-2015/.

'US kids spend too much time in front of a screen and too little asleep, study finds', *The Guardian* (27 September 2018), at https://www.theguardian.com/us-news/2018/sep/27/us-children-sleep-screen-time-cognitive-skills-study.

Twenge, Jean M., interviewed in Frank Miniter, 'Are Smartphones Killing Teens'. *Forbes* (21 November 2017), at https://www.forbes.com/sites/frankminiter/2017/11/21/are-smartphones-killing-teens/.

Twenge, Jean M., and W. Keith Campbell. 'Associations Between Screen Time and Lower Psychological Well-Being Among Children and Adolescents'. *Preventive Medicine Reports* 12 (2018), at https://doi.org/10.1016/j.pmedr.2018.10.003.

Wang, Youfa, and Hyunjung Lim. 'The Global Childhood Obesity Epidemic'. *International Review of Psychiatry* 24, no.3 (2012), at https://doi.org/10.3109/09540261.2012.688195.

Printed in Great Britain
by Amazon

42748037R00064